DATE DUE

OCT 2 8 1995	
Nov 4	
FEB -7 1996	
FEB 1 2 1996	
FEB 2 6 1996	
JAN 2 3 1997	
JAN 3 1 1998	
Feb 13	
SEP 3 0 1999	
DEC 1 4 1999	
MAY - 2 2000	

BRODART   Cat. No. 23-221

Controversial
Issues in
Health Care
Policy

CONTROVERSIAL ISSUES IN PUBLIC POLICY

Series Editors
Dennis Palumbo and Rita Mae Kelly
Arizona State University

Controversial Issues in Health Care Policy

Jennie J. Kronenfeld

Controversial Issues in Public Policy
Volume 5

SAGE Publications
International Educational and Professional Publisher
Newbury Park   London   New Delhi

For information address:

 SAGE Publications, Inc.
2455 Teller Road
Newbury Park, California 91320

SAGE Publications Ltd.
6 Bonhill Street
London EC2A 4PU
United Kingdom

SAGE Publications India Pvt. Ltd.
M-32 Market
Greater Kailash I
New Delhi 110 048 India

Printed in the United States of America

Library of Congress Cataloging-in-Publication Data

Kronenfeld, Jennie Jacobs
    Controversial issues in health care policy / Jennie Jacobs Kronenfeld.
        p.   cm.—(Controversial issues in public policy ; 5)
    Includes bibliographical references and index.
    ISBN 0-8039-4877-8.—ISBN 0-8039-4878-6 (pbk.)
    1. Medical policy—United States. I. Title. II. Series,
RA395.A3K758   1993
362.1'0973—dc20   92-35472
                                                                  CIP

93 94 95 96   10 9 8 7 6 5 4 3 2 1

Sage Production Editor: Judith L. Hunter

Contents

Series Editors' Introduction

Public policy controversies escalated during the 1980s and early 1990s. This was partly due to bitter partisan debate between Republicans and Democrats, a "divided" government in which the Republicans controlled the presidency and the Democrats controlled the Congress, and the rise of negative campaigning in the 1988 presidential election. In addition, the past decade was a time when highly controversial issues such as abortion, crime, environmental pollution, affirmative action, and choice in education became prominent on the public policy agenda.

Policy issues in this atmosphere tend to be framed in dichotomous, either/or terms. Abortion is depicted as "murder" on the one hand, or a woman's "self-interested choice" on the other. One is either "tough on crime," or too much in favor of "defendants' rights." Affirmative action is a matter of quotas for correcting the "educational mess," or the destruction of public education. In such a situation there does not seem to be a middle or common ground where cooler heads can unite.

The shrillness of these policy disputes reduces the emphasis on finding rational, balanced solutions. Political ideology and a zero-sum approach to politics and policy become the order of the day.

Certainly, there hasn't been an "end to ideology" over the past decade and a half, as some have believed was occurring in the 1970s. "Reaganomics" contributed to a widening gap between the rich and the poor during the 1980s and this seemed to exacerbate partisan debate and further stymie governmental action. In 1992 controversies over health care—not only lack of coverage for millions but also skyrocketing costs—illustrate the wide gap in the way Republicans and Democrats approach public policy controversies. The Reagan "revolution" was based on a definite and clear ideological preference for a certain approach to public policy in general: eliminate government regulation; reduce taxes; provide tax incentives for business; cut welfare; and privatize the delivery of governmental services. Democrats, of course, did not agree.

This series in Public Policy Controversies is meant to shed more light and less ideological heat on major policy issues in the substantive policy areas. In this volume Kronenfeld covers controversial issues ranging from AIDS to abortion, aging, costs, mental health, and health care providers. She begins by noting that the United States spends more on health care than all other countries, yet we have between 33 and 38 million Americans who have no health insurance. Even though the United States has the most advanced medical technology in the world, it ranks 19th among nations in infant mortality.

In order to answer why this is the case, Kronenfeld first describes the three different health care systems (or non-systems) in the United States and the various controversies associated with them. In order to improve the systems it is necessary to be able to measure and define health, which she addresses in Chapter 2. Of course, no matter how it is measured, health is related to income level and, surprisingly, not necessarily to the availability of medical services. In fact, in the area of mental health, less availability was considered best in the deinstitutionalization movement, when hundreds of thousands of mentally ill patients were released from state and county mental health institutions.

Birth control and abortion are two of the more controversial issues taken up by Kronenfeld, especially as they are related to the epidemic of teenage pregnancies in the United States. These are areas that are extremely emotional and therefore difficult to find adequate remedies for. Another, considered by Kronenfeld in Chapter 5, is aging. As the U.S. population grows older, the cost of health care will inevitably go up because the largest proportion of health care expenditures goes to the elderly. However, in 1992, the United States still did not have a satisfactory policy or program for long-term care for the elderly.

This volume sheds a great deal of light on these and many other crucial issues in health care. This is a policy area that will become increasingly important in the coming years. Readers of this volume will be well equipped to understand and perhaps contribute to solutions for these complex problems.

RITA MAE KELLY
DENNIS PALUMBO

Acknowledgments

I would like to thank many people for assistance in writing this book. My department chair, Howard Zuckerman, was particularly helpful at the end in arranging to have the typing of tables completed. Valerie Hedges, my graduate assistant provided by the School of Health Administration and Policy, was very helpful in researching the facts and figures needed for the book. Janet Soter of the College of Public Programs was most helpful in producing the figures for this book. Also, Rita Mae Kelly and Dennis Palumbo were helpful in their roles as series editors.

I would also like to thank my family. My husband, Michael Kronenfeld, was understanding and patient in his personal role about the time needed to write this book. He also helped in his professional role as a librarian with provision of some of the needed materials and tabular data, as well as in reading the entire manuscript. My three children, Shaun, Jeffrey, and Aaron, were patient much of the time as concerns the time demands and very pleased when their mother appeared less frantic since the book was completed to coincide with the occurrence of their summer vacations. Last, I would like to acknowledge my mother, Bessie Jacobs, whose intellectual stimulation and encouragement have been important at all stages of my career, but especially when I was in high school and college.

1

Introduction to
Health Care Policy Issues

One hundred years ago, few people ever spoke about health care. Back in 1883, going to the hospital was a rare (and dreaded) event in most people's lives. Going to the doctor was something people did infrequently, usually only when they saw no other recourse for feeling better and getting back to work. In the past 35 years, all of this has changed for the average, middle-class American. Health care in the United States has grown into a multibillion-dollar industry. Health care related stocks and companies have experienced rapid growth and large gains in value during the late 1980s and early 1990s. People do not dread going to a hospital, although fewer people spend the night in one now than 30 years ago (mostly because so many types of health care that used to require a long hospital stay now can be done in one day, with the patient returning home to his or her own bed). But going to the doctor is a more common event, something people do when they feel fine as well as when they feel sick. Increasingly, people go to the doctor to help them stay well, such as through a general physical examination, and to prevent new problems from developing. Thus many, and probably most, Americans view access to health care as important. They see their own health care as generally effective and take pride in the excellent medical care technology and up-to-date, technologically sophisticated hospitals that are found across the United States.

Moreover, many experts now agree that the United States health care system has been successful in achieving the most technologically advanced medical care system in the world and that most of this technology is available to affluent and middle-lass consumers of health care services (Botehlo, 1991; Todd, Seekins, Kirchbaum, & Harvey, 1991). Moreover, the United States has become the premier nation among all nations in the provision of high-quality, comprehensive medical education (Todd et al.). Physicians come from all over the world to receive the most advanced and sophisticated training and learn how to use the newest medical equipment.

Based on this glowing description of a larger, more important, and more comprehensive health care system (especially as regards technologically oriented care), you might conclude that health care has been one of the great American success stories. People must be healthier than in the past and get care whenever they need it. Quality must be high, and costs reasonable, or how could health care have grown into a major industry? Unfortunately, such is not the case. While each decade for the past 30 years at least has had some discussion of a "health care crisis," making this a most overused phrase, current descriptions of problems and crises in the U.S. health care system abound.

In May 1991 the American Medical Association, the largest association of physicians of various specialties across the United States, published special issues of most of its major journals, including its overall publication for all physicians, *Journal of the American Medical Association* (*JAMA*), focusing on caring for the uninsured and underinsured. One article in *JAMA*, titled "Caring for the Uninsured," pointed out that a national commission on medicine and ethical problems in 1983 had concluded that society has a moral obligation to ensure that everyone in the United States has access to adequate health care (Menken, 1991; President's Commission, 1983). Judging by this standard, Menken concluded that the health system of the United States is failing. Menken's conclusion was based on a series of statistics and facts about the current health care system in the United States.

What are some of the facts about the current U.S. health care system that lead to terms such as *crisis* and *failure*? Between 33 and 38 million citizens are uninsured and thus unable to receive health care when it is needed. Worse yet, many of these people without health insurance (probably about 26 million) are working Americans and their families, not the unemployed or those on public assistance. About 11 million of those without health insurance are children. These large numbers of uninsured occur despite the fact that in 1990 the United States spent more than $662 billion, or 12.2% of the gross national product, on health care. If we try to relate this huge figure to individuals, that is enough to spend an average of $2,566 per person in the United States on health care for that year. Compared to almost all other countries, the United States is a high spender on health care. The United States spends 38% more per capita on health care costs than does Canada, 88% more than West Germany, and 124% more than Japan, to compare the United States to three large, industrialized countries with good health care systems and a healthy population. Thus these other countries spend less on health care and yet cover their total population more comprehensively than does the United States.

Why does the United States spend more and yet have more people not covered by health insurance? Is it because our health care is better than in other countries? There is not one simple answer to this very important policy question because what we mean by *better* when we discuss health care is not always clear. As already mentioned, the United States does tend to have available the most technologically sophisticated health care. The United States also typically has this technologically sophisticated care available in larger quantities than in other countries and frequently has it first because it was developed in the United States. The United States is a leader in the development of new medical technology and in medical education. Thus if being better means more technology and better technical training, the United States is among the best. But if being either better or the best means having the healthiest population in the world, then clearly the United States does not have the best health care. In fact, on many of the indicators typically used to rank countries on health status, the United States does not do as well as one would expect for a country of its wealth, education, and technological sophistication.

One of the most reported comparative health indicators is the infant mortality rate, the number of babies who die in the first year of life. The U.S. figure was 10.4 per 1,000 live births in 1985, which placed the United States 19th among the nations. The U.S. rate has been improving, and provisional figures for 1988 were about 10. Japan had the lowest infant mortality rate, 5.5 per 1,000 live births. Most Western European countries such as Sweden, West Germany before the merger of the east and west, Great Britain, and the Netherlands all had lower infant mortality rates than the United States.

One common explanation given for the higher infant mortality rate in the United States is that it is a more diverse country than many others, and that it has a greater number of new immigrants. Although this is true, as compared to a country such as Japan or Sweden, it is not the only explanation. A related explanation is that the United States has more poor people than some of the other countries, and infant mortality rates are typically higher in poor populations. One of the important linkages between poverty and higher infant mortality rates is less and later use of prenatal care, and this is one of the explanations for higher rates of infant mortality in the United States.

Which explanation is correct? Several different sets of answers to these explanations are important. While the United States is a much more diverse and ethnically complex country than some of the countries with the lowest infant mortality rates (such as Sweden and Japan), ethnic mix is at best a partial answer. For example, not all recent immigrants to the United States have higher infant mortality rates. In fact, among Hispanics of Mexican-American origin, recent immigrants to the United States often have lower infant mortality rates than those in the next generation.

What about the issue of linkages between the numbers of poor and lower infant health? One of the best approaches to trying to understand why U.S. infant mortality rates are higher would involve computation of the infant mortality rate in the United States only for wealthier or non-poor Americans and seeing how that figure compares to figures from other countries. Unfortunately, such data are not available on any systematic basis since most data on birth and death rates come from aggregation of state statistics from birth and death records that have not generally included information on income. Given the strong association in the United States at this point in time between race/ethnic status and income (and the overall policy importance of examining differentials in infant mortality rates by race), one simplified way to compare infant mortality rates for income groups is to compare the figures for whites and blacks. While not perfect, this comparison involves data which are easier to obtain since the race of the mother has been recorded on most state birth certificates for many years. Only in the past few years have many states begun to add information about education (and, less frequently, income) to state birth certificate forms. The infant mortality rate for black infants is about twice that of white infants (18.0 for blacks versus 8.9 for whites in 1986). Thus the U.S. rate would be lower if the country had less ethnic diversity and had fewer poor people. It is also probably correct that if poorer people had better access to health care, their rates would decrease some. Among blacks in 1986, only 61% received prenatal care in the first 3 months of pregnancy, versus about

80% among whites. But the racial and ethnic diversity of the United States is not the only explanation for higher infant mortality rates in the United States, since even the U.S. white rate of 8.9 is substantially higher than the best foreign rate (Japan at 5.5). Thus, as measured by infant mortality rates, the United States does not have a better health care system, despite spending more money on health care.

How does the typical American now view health care? Do middle-class people with good health insurance coverage see the health care system as working well? A recent public opinion poll, conducted in 10 different counties, found that the United States ranked the lowest in the percentage of respondents who agreed with the statement: "On the whole, our health system works pretty well and only minor changes are necessary to make it work better." In fact, the largest group of Americans, about 60%, agreed with the statement: "There are some good things in our health care system, but fundamental changes are needed to make it work better." Thirty percent felt there was so much wrong with the U.S. health care system that it needed to be completely rebuilt (Blendon, 1990). A recent special election for a Senate seat in Pennsylvania (necessary due to the death of the former senator) focused a great deal on health care, with the Democratic candidate, Wofford, winning an upset victory based on his advocacy of health care system reform. Given this increasing percentage of Americans who believe there are many problems with the U.S. health care system (as evidenced by polling data and some election data), one focus of this book will be to describe aspects of the current system and focus on the most important policy issues. There are a large number of different types of proposals to change the health care system, and experts vary greatly on which they believe is most likely to be politically feasible (Reinhardt, 1991). Before beginning a discussion of specific policies, however, we need more discussion of the current U.S. health care system.

Is There a National Health Care System and National Health Care Policy?

One interesting complication when trying to compare the health care system in the United States to those in other countries is trying to determine what the system is. In reality, there is no one health care system in the United States, but many. One major text in health administration argues that the United States has a number of different subsystems and describes four major ones (Torrens, 1988). These four are: (a) systems that serve regularly employed, middle-income and up families with continuous and fairly comprehensive health insurance coverage; (b) the system that serves poor, unemployed (or underemployed) families without continuous health insurance coverage; (c) the system that serves active duty U.S. military personnel and their dependents; and (d) the system that serves veterans of U.S. military service (Torrens).

The latter two of these systems would fit most definitions of a system of care, that is, there is an organized way for patients to enter into health care, to be transferred into a hospital if there are such needs, and to receive rehabilitation services or other special services. Generally, these latter two are national systems that operate all across the country, and with many similarities as one goes from place to place.

In contrast, the first two subsystems as described are themselves composed not of one unified system, which is the same from one place in the United States to another, but rather of a series of different sequences of care that people manage to pull together. For most Americans, these subsystems are still an informal set of services that each individual or family puts together. The private practice physician is typically the core of this system, particularly for the middle-class system, and often people will have a number of different physicians from whom they receive care. These different physicians often may not know each other or even formally communicate. Thus each patient, in some ways, creates his or her own system. This model is usually financed by insurance obtained through the workplace and, for the middle-class person, by out-of-pocket payments. One more recent variant of this system is the HMO, or health maintenance organization, in which a more unified system of care or set of providers is already organized as part of the health insurance and financing arrangement.

For the poor or those not continuously insured, the system is likely to include a mixture of private physicians, hospital emergency rooms and outpatient clinics, and county health department clinics through the local county or city public health care system. This model is usually paid for by some limited out-of-pocket payments, but mostly by governmentally financed care or charity care donated by a health care facility or physicians. For the poor eligible for Medicaid, there are actually 50 different systems of health care delivery because each state has some flexibility in determining both eligibility levels for the poor and the range of services to be covered.

For a growing number of American families, another approach (particularly for the middle-class system of care) to obtaining and paying for health care services is a more formal arrangement of types of services, often called an HMO (health maintenance organization), a PPO (preferred provider organization), or a managed care plan. For the past 20 years, group practice reimbursed on a prepaid rather than fee-for-service basis (fee paid at the time for each particular visit or service the patient receives) has been called an HMO and often included the notion of physicians practicing together under one roof, with many different specialties represented. In the past 10 years, many other arrangements that include prepayment and management of care patterns have arisen. These include IPAs (independent practice associations or plans), in which community-based solo and group practitioners join together with a health insurance company to provide a preset group of health care services, and PPOs, which are very similar but with strong ties to a particular insurer and usually a particular hospital as the site of inpatient (overnight) care. *Managed care* is a term used in the past 5 or so years that describes attempts to control use of services, to require prechecking with the insurance company before certain procedures or surgeries are done, and to help an individual coordinate care. HMOs, PPOs, and IPAs all are examples of managed care in today's health care environment. Most forms of prepayment and managed care plans have achieved lower costs for total care, often particularly through reduced hospital utilization, and hospital rates that are lower than in the fee-for-service sector (Cascardo, 1982; Hoy, Curtis, & Rice, 1991; Robinson, 1991). These types of health care delivery arrangements are growing, however. Reasons for their growth include both the ability to help control rising health care costs (a particular concern for employers, who have been switching to such systems of health care insurance and away from traditional fee-for-service plans) and the ability to help consumers create a more integrated and comprehensive system of heath care delivery, although at the expense of some individual choice. Some states now require a form of managed care for the recipients of Medicaid, the jointly financed state/federal health insurance program for the poor.

There are further complexities in the basic systems. The creation of the Medicare program (formally Title 18 of the Social Security Act) in 1965 to provide federal health insurance for the elderly means that even middle-class people over 65 partially participate in a federally provided system of care. While initially this system operated very similarly to the fee-for-service system, it now has its own special means of paying hospitals and is about to implement a revised set of fee schedules for paying physicians. Given the size of the Medicare system (covering almost all people over 65 and those under 65 with certain kidney problems or certain serious disabilities), revisions in ways to pay hospitals and doctors that are begun in the Medicare program quickly become an issue of public discussion and, at times, are extended to other payor groups.

For the poor and the uninsured, there are also several different subsystems operating. Many poor individuals (from 35% to 60%, depending upon the state) receive health care through the Medicaid program (formally Title 19 of the Social Security Act), the federal/state cooperative health care program for the categorically eligible poor and for certain other specific groups of poor individuals. Because Medicaid is a joint program between the states and the federal government, an examination of it helps to clarify one way in which the United States does not have just one single health care system. Although there are federal requirements as to groups of the poor who must be provided Medicaid coverage (often termed the federally mandated), and similarly a list of federally mandated services that must be provided, states have flexibility in establishing the amount of income and resources a person can have and still qualify for the Medicaid program in that state. Similarly, some states cover almost all physician care and much dental and eye care, while others cover no dental or eye care and even specify the number of medications a person can obtain each month, such as a limit of three.

One argument about health care policy in the United States in the 1960s and 1970s was that there is no "system" of care, but rather a non-system. Part of this argument stressed the waste and inefficiency overall in a situation in which there are many competing models of care. A related criticism is that in many of the largest U.S. cities, there are competing systems of care connected with different medical schools, such as one finds in New York City, Chicago, and Los Angeles. These were labeled "health care empires" and are viewed by one group of critics as one major explanation for inefficient, costly care because each "empire" duplicates expensive services and competes to attract patients (Health-PAC, 1970).

Although the non-system and competing systems of care approaches were major critiques of the U.S. health care system 20 years ago, different arguments and critiques were heard after the Reagan administration took over in 1980. Particularly important was a concern about the lack of competition, and especially price-based competition by health care providers. The essence of this argument is based on free market economic theory and argues that competition in the provision of any goods or service is important in keeping the cost of that service reasonable. Thus one policy implication of this approach is to create increased competition in health care. If we accept a competitive model of health care, perhaps all of these multiple systems of care, including the competing medical care empires controlled by different medical schools critiqued in the 1960s, are actually a good feature of our health care system. Much disagreement exists both among health care policy experts and among politicians about the best approach to structuring an improved health care delivery system. While there are some enthusiastic proponents of such an approach (Enthoven, 1980; Enthoven & Kronick, 1989, 1991), most health care policy experts agree there are a number of problems and limitations with a multiple competing systems model of health care delivery. One of the most important limitations is the growing conviction that in a system with multiple competing models, and thus competition for resources, the stronger, more aggressive, and better connected health care consumers will obtain more, and others will obtain less. Thus, the middle-class system, the military system, and even the VA (Veterans Administration) systems have obtained more resources and technology than have the systems for the poor. Moreover, this competition for resources often results in wasteful duplication and inefficient utilization of resources, partially the argument of the non-system critics of the 1960s. A difference today is that while 30 years ago, many policy experts were willing to argue that the United States was a wealthy enough country to afford duplication and waste if such a system was the preferred model of care for many Americans, most experts and businesspeople today are concerned with the cost of health care and its impact on the overall competitiveness of American industry and products in a global economy.

Just as, in the case of health care systems, it is not clear that there is only one system operating, this is also true about health care policy. Is there one health care policy operating across the entire country, or do other factors, such as state lines, create multiple policy-making levels in health care? This is a particular concern for the Medicaid program, the major payor of health care for the poor, because it is very much connected with state-level policy decisions. Moreover, not all of the poor who are covered by Medicaid are those who we commonly think of as the long-term poor (people who have been on public assistance much of their lives and have rarely worked steadily at a job). Rather, because the Medicare program for the elderly provides only very limited coverage for long-term care services (such as nursing home care), and because nursing home care is so expensive that most people run out of funds to pay for it themselves, many elderly people who were not poor most of their lives end up as Medicaid clients if they require nursing home care as they age. In fact, in most states, about half the Medicaid budget goes to provide nursing home and long-term care services for the elderly. As already explained, the Medicaid program is not one federal program but rather a series of 50 different programs with many different requirements and regulations. Thus, that aspect of health policy is not handled simply at the federal level.

In addition, the majority of funds for mental health care services (or behavioral health care services) in the United States is provided not from private insurance or federal funds, but from state funds, so states play a major role in determining policy in the mental health area. Many publicly supported hospitals are county hospitals that are paid for from county tax revenues. Decisions about changes in access and services thus involve county supervisors and boards, in addition to state legislatures and the U.S. Congress. Most medical school education and nursing education is provided in state-supported medical schools and universities. While over the past 30 years, the federal government has provided subsidies to states in the form of capitation grants to help pay for education in the health professions, state funds are nevertheless a major source for such schools, and thus policy about the availability of health personnel is also determined at many levels.

Politics and the Health Policy Process

A nation's health policy is part of its general overall social policy. As such, health policy formulation is influenced by the variety and array of social and economic factors that impact on broader policy development issues in the United States. The nature and history of existing institutions, ritualized methods for dealing with social conflict, and general goals and values of a society all play a role in the formulation of such policy.

An important overall factor is the basic ideological orientation of the United States. There are two aspects of this: the economic system of capitalism and the political orientation of classical liberalism or perhaps, given the usage today of conservative and liberal as descriptors of sides of the political spectrum, individualism.

Classical liberalism or individualism emphasizes individuals as the basis and justification for the creation of government. Most things affecting individual well-being, including responsibility for personal health care, are to be both the choice and the responsibility of the individual. Capitalism emphasizes the operation of a free market economy and competition. Combined with this is a belief that society would be better off as a whole if each individual within it vigorously pursued his or her welfare to the greatest extent possible.

Only in the twentieth century in the United States has there been a view of government as a counterweight to other powerful forces in the society, and the provider of last resort for certain types of services. Government began to be regarded as the provider of public goods/services for overall well-being, which, for various reasons, were provided within the context of the private marketplace.

Given this orientation, the provision of health care services has traditionally been provided through a competitive marketplace. Only since 1964 has the federal government played a more major role in the provision of health care services to certain specialized groups, such as some of the poor and the elderly. Currently, the United States is engaged in a policy debate over how to extend at least minimal health care services to all, and whether the provision of these services will continue as part of a private market, a subsidized market, or a national health care system. As this book explores various policy options in health care, it will be useful to remember the traditional political and economic philosophical orientation of the United States. Many parts of the current debate relate back to these basic issues of how one views government and the role of government and the individual.

The Big Three of Health Services Research

What do the facts and figures about health care begin to make us conclude about health care policy and future health care related controversies in the United States? They tell us that access to health care is a major controversy, costs and financing of health care (how we pay for care) is another one, and quality of health care is a third.

Cost, quality, and access have been the three key watchwords for scholars in many of the different disciplines that study health care and the delivery of health care services. The name given to these types of studies and studies related to many aspects of the health care system is *health services research.* This name began being used about 25 years ago to describe research related to the use of, organization and delivery of, financing of, and outcomes of health services such as quality of care and health status changes. Over the past 10 years, it has become the most widely accepted term to describe interdisciplinary research on health and health care services. Disciplines that are often part of health services research include sociology, economics, political science, management sciences, epidemiology, and more applied fields such as public health, health services administration, health education, and policy sciences. That interstitial area between policy sciences and health care studies is the focus of this book. Cost of health care services, quality of those services, and access to those services are the three critical issues of health care policy and are cross-cutting issues that are addressed in the last three chapters of this book, Chapters 7, 8, and 9.

The importance of these three controversies (cost, quality, and access) should not be surprising, and actually would be true for many kinds of services that a person might receive, not just health care. For any service (or product), one thing of importance is, how much does it cost? For an individual about to visit a doctor (or a store), the simple question is, what must I pay? The more complicated question is whether the price is fair, reasonable, and appropriate. When this question is applied beyond the individual to a large group or to the nation as a whole, we begin to ask questions such as, what are the total dollars being spent, how do these dollars relate to other kinds of services, and how do they relate to how much people in other places pay for these kinds of services?

A related question is, can I get the service or product? This is the question of access. Access has at least two components, one of which is simply the availability of the service. Are there doctors or hospitals around? Are the doctors taking new patients? Do the hospitals have empty beds? In health care, this question is often termed *geographical access* and is linked to specific places. While the answers to policy questions about geographical access can be complex, the more complex side is *financial access,* or do I have the money to pay for care? Increasingly in the United States, the answer to this question relates less to the amount of money any individual has in his or her wallet or bank account, and more to whether the person (and the person's family) has health insurance. The most important factor in having health insurance in the United States today is having a good job with benefits. In addition, certain categories of people, such as the elderly, now have access to governmentally sponsored health insurance. Thus, access for an individual is partially linked to cost of care and partially linked to specific aspects of that person's situation in the society.

Moving beyond the individual to the society as a whole, cost of care is linked to access, and at a broader policy level, this is particularly true. If a governmental unit, such as a state, is willing to spend a certain amount of dollars on health care for the poor and those without insurance, the state can provide more access to care to greater numbers of people if the average cost of care per person is $500 instead of $1,000. Thus, as a public policy controversy, costs and access are important and interrelated.

The third controversy concerning quality of care is again a question we would ask about any type of service or even a specific product to be purchased. Is it a quality product, or is the care I will receive of high quality? Is it at least of acceptable quality? For consumer products, we often trade off between quality and cost. People decide to accept a less well-made product (one that may not last as long) if the price is lower. Once we begin to talk about a service such as health care, which involves the person's body and possible life or death consequences, many people adopt the attitude that only the best quality is acceptable. But what is the best quality, and are we always able to measure quality in health care? These are important policy controversies and they quickly become interwoven with policy about cost and access. That the government and individuals should not pay for inferior quality health care is a statement with which almost everyone agrees. But must everyone have the most technologically sophisticated care for it to be of high quality? The phrases *two-tiered* or *two-class* system of care have often been used to describe aspects of U.S. health care in the past, with one tier or class for individually (and insured) paying patients, and another for charity (or more recently, governmentally funded) patients. Is this acceptable, and is providing different levels of quality of care still an appropriate way to provide access to all? Clearly, quality becomes a third major consideration, along with cost and access.

Health Status, Age Groups, and Specific Health Problems

Not all public policy issues relating to health deal with the controversies surrounding cost, quality, and access. Another whole area of health care policy concerns health status and specific types of health

care to address those health problems. Many issues of policy importance concern ways to use public policy to improve the health of all
Americans or to reduce differentials in health between different groups
of citizens. Related policy controversies concern specific diseases and
especially the impact of new diseases, such as AIDS. Nor is health care
policy restricted only to physical health concerns. One major area of
expenditure of public funds for health is in the area of mental health or
what is today often called behavioral health. This can include care for
mental health problems, such as depression or schizophrenia, as well as
care for such behavioral problems as alcohol and drug abuse.

A third major area of policy debate within the United States over the
past 20 to 30 years has related to reproductive health concerns, including control of fertility, lack of fertility, and abortion as one method to
control fertility. There are several reasons why this particular specialized area of health care has taken on such importance. One reason is
because the health of a nation's babies is one of the most important
indicators of overall health status, as indicated in the above discussion
of infant mortality statistics. Another reason has been that the nature of
the policy debate in this area has become somewhat different from that
in some other health policy areas. Issues of morality and strongly held
beliefs about the sanctity of life and when life begins are major controversies within this policy area. Given the unique nature of the public
policy debate on this topic, this area of health policy is important
enough to deserve separate examination. Thus these three areas (diseases relating to physical health and health care, behavioral health
concerns, and reproductive health concerns) are the focus of the next
three chapters in this book, Chapters 2, 3, and 4.

Another major health policy area—aging and long-term care—relates
both to diseases and to health care delivery. The elderly are the most rapidly
growing sector of the U.S. population. While at the turn of the century only
about 4% of the U.S. population was 65 or older, about 12% of the
population is in this age category currently (Pepper Commission, 1990).
As the baby boomers (the large population group born between 1946 and
1964) age, the percentage 65 and older will increase, making up perhaps
as much as 20% of the population, depending on birth rates over the next
20 years. Older people, especially those 75 and over, require more health
and social services than the general population. They are also the largest
users of long-term care services, such as nursing home care and home
health care. Thus another important set of health policy controversies,
relating to aging and long-term care services, is covered in Chapter 5.

Health Resources

One common description of delivery of health care services is that it involves an interaction between two parties: the consumer or user of care and the deliverer or provider of care. Chapter 6 will focus on policy relating to providers of health care services, both people and institutions. One portion of the chapter will focus on both the people who deliver health care services and policies relating to numbers of such personnel, how they are trained, and how they are paid. Obviously, many of these controversies, especially payment of providers, will also be addressed in other chapters because these aspects of health policy cannot be considered in isolation.

Health care providers include physicians, the group that has the most power and receives the largest financial reward within the system; nurses, the largest group of providers; and an entire array of allied health care providers. This chapter will explore policy issues relating to planning for the number of such personnel, training these people, and how they are paid as well as how they interact with each other.

Health care institutions include hospitals, managed care organizations, and all types of specialized outpatient care facilities. Nursing homes are an example of another type of health care institution, but policy relating to these facilities is so tied in with policy issues about the elderly that it will be discussed in Chapter 5. There are a very large number of policy controversies that relate to health care institutions. Part of this chapter will cover changes in the organization and function of hospitals and changes in hospital reimbursement policy, policy issues relating to the providing of funds to build or improve health care institutions (capital financing), and special problems of provision of health care institutions in rural parts of the United States. Growth of managed care plans and outpatient facilities will also be discussed, although these issues link with the policy decisions that must be made about ways to provide access to health care services.

Cost, Quality, and Access

As already mentioned, these are the three overarching themes in health services research and they have already been explained earlier in this chapter. The last three chapters of this book will focus on these three areas, with Chapter 7 exploring costs and associated controversies, Chapter 8 exploring quality and associated controversies, and

Chapter 9 exploring access and plans to reform the U.S. health care system. These three areas cover what are likely to be both the most important and the most controversial areas in the next 10 years. The concluding portion of Chapter 9 will review the many proposals to reform the U.S. health care system and discuss the possibilities for major reform in the next decade.

2

Disease Patterns, Physical Health, and AIDS

Obviously one important part of health policy relates to how to improve the health status of the population. Thus one important goal of any national health policy is to improve health and well-being of the citizens of that country. As soon as we make such a statement, the next questions are: How is the health of a nation defined, and how will improvements in health be measured? Defining health has long been a thorny problem for analysts of the health care system.

A very traditional way to define health has been as the absence of disease or illness. This has become known as the negative definition of health. It is a negative approach both because it is a limited definition and, more important, because it does not say what health is, but rather what the negative of health is. Another aspect of why that traditional definition is limited is because it has an almost exclusive focus on physical health status. The definition pays little attention to mental and behavioral health and ignores social health. To meet these criticisms of the traditional definition of health, WHO (World Health Organization, the health arm of the United Nations) adopted a broadened definition of health in the early 1950s. The WHO definition not only stressed the absence of disease, but also included an emphasis on nonphysical aspects of the quality of life. This expanded definition includes a tripartite conceptualization of an individual's total ability to function in his or her relevant environment, including physical, mental, and social dimensions (WHO, 1958). At the time this broadened definition was first proposed, it was quite controversial, although over the past 30 years many nations have gradually broadened their health policy focus to be more in line with the expanded definition.

Conceptualizing and defining health continues to plague health policy makers and researchers. Even the expanded definition is only a starting point and does not lend itself quickly and easily to the measurement and following of trends for setting policy goals. Over the past 30 years, some researchers have focused on the concept of functional limitations and have broken the dimensions of health into categories such as physical health, self-care activities, social role activities, and mobility (Haber, 1966; Patrick, Bush, & Chen, 1973; Reynolds, Rushing, & Miles, 1974). A different way of conceptualizing health is Schlenger's (1976) two-dimensional model. One dimension is the traditional absence of disease. The second dimension emphasizes the affective or feeling aspects of health. For example, a person with terminal disease (such as one dying of cancer) would clearly have very poor health in terms of the absence of disease dimension. Yet some cancer patients might rank high on the affective dimension of health by having accepted the reality of their situation and having dealt positively with that reality and the use of the time they have left.

Even if all health policy experts were to agree on a single definition of health, the data collection required to obtain all of this information would represent a massive and extremely complicated undertaking. Many studies have tried to define readily employable measurement instruments through which health data could be easily obtained. Most of these attempts employ population and community surveys to avoid sole reliance on physician obtained data (and thus a bias that only people who actually make it to a health care provider would be included). Any accurate measure of the overall health of a country must be based on the total population, not just those who use health care, visit social service facilities, or are well integrated into society. Indeed, there is evidence that those who are not well integrated into the social fabric of a society (such as the homeless) may be groups in which health status is particularly poor.

In addition to being sure to measure the health of everyone and thinking of many broad definitions of health, these definitions must be translated into specific scales and ways to collect data. While no single instrument has become the one measure of health, several multidimensional approaches have been developed to capture physical, mental, and social well-being (Patrick et al., 1973; Renne, 1974; Reynolds et al., 1976; Williams, Johnston, Willis, & Bennett, 1976). Recently one entire book has been devoted to categorizing the various measures of health (McDowell & Newell, 1987). Bergner and Rothman (1987) provide a systematic review and critique of major multi-item health status measures. Most approaches now include the use of multidimensional survey data, simple questions asking a person to rate his or her own health; physician based assessments of health status, often linked to the presence or absence of major chronic illnesses; and aggregate population measures such as infant mortality rate, average life expectancy, and amount of disability in a population.

Health Status in the Past and Now

How healthy are Americans today, and are levels of health similar for most people? If we think back to our comparison of the health care system of 100 years ago with the one today, and compare the U.S. population on diseases and health status, there have been major shifts in the most important causes of death and in overall rates of death. Reliable data on causes of death in the United States did not begin to become available until 1900. Between 1900 and 1973, there was almost a 70% decline in overall mortality. Of the total fall in death rates in this time period, most (about 92%) occurred prior to 1950.

What were the major diseases and health problems due to which people were dying in each time period? In 1900 about 40% of all deaths were accounted for by 11 major infectious diseases (typhoid, smallpox, scarlet fever, measles, whooping cough, diphtheria, influenza, tuberculosis, pneumonia, disease of the digestive system, and poliomyelitis), 16% by three major chronic conditions (heart disease, cancer, and stroke), and 4% by accidents, leaving 37% for an assortment of all other causes (McKinlay & McKinlay, 1977). By 1973 the percentage of deaths due to infectious diseases had declined to only 6%, while the percentage due to chronic conditions such as cancer and heart disease had increased to 58%. Deaths due to accidents were also up, to 9%, and the percentage of deaths from all other causes in 1977 was 27%. The most important explanation for the decline in deaths is the virtual

Table 2.1 Trends in Death Rates, 1920-1987

Death rates and causes (per 100,000 population)	1920	1940	1960	1980	1987
Death rates	1,298.9	1,076.4	954.7	874.1	872.4
Major causes of death					
Pneumonia and influenza	207.3	70.3	37.3	23.2	28.4
Diseases of the heart	159.6	292.5	369.0	335.9	312.4
Tuberculosis	113.1	45.9	6.1	*	*
Cerebrovascular diseases	93.0	90.9	108.0	75.0	61.6
Malignant neoplasms	83.4	120.3	149.2	182.4	195.9
Accidents	71.0	73.6	52.3	46.9	39.0
Infant mortality (per 1,000 live births)	NA	47.0	26.0	12.5	10.1
Maternal mortality (per 100,000 live births)	NA	376.0	37.1	6.9	6.6

*Not listed as a major cause of death.
SOURCE: National Center for Health Statistics, *Monthly Vital Statistics Report*, September 26, 1989.

disappearance of deaths due to the traditional infectious diseases. Table 2.1 shows the trends in death rates in the United States from 1920 through 1987, and the large decline in major infectious causes such as pneumonia and tuberculosis is quite striking, in contrast to heart-related ailments and neoplasms or cancer.

A different analysis has compared age-adjusted death rates for the five leading causes of death in 1900 in 10 states, and in 1977 for the total United States (National Center for Health Statistics, 1980). Again a major shift away from the importance of infectious diseases occurred, reflecting successes in sanitary engineering and general standards of living as well as in medical care and technology. In 1977 heart disease accounted for 2 in 5 deaths, cancer for 1 in 5, and accidents for 1 in 10. If we think not only of causes of death but also of the impact of the leading causes of death on years of lost life, we find that heart disease and cancer accounted for a smaller proportion of lost years than of death, because these two diseases strike with higher frequency in older age groups. In contrast, accidents account for almost twice as high a proportion of years of lost life as deaths because children, teenagers, and young adults are the most important numerically as victims of accidents and violence.

In the most recent mortality statistics, three out of four deaths in the United States are caused by the four leading causes of death: diseases of the heart, cancer, stroke or cerebrovascular disease, and accidents and adverse effects. Two of these, heart disease and stroke, however, have been in a pattern of long-term decline although they still remain among the four leading causes of death (National Center for Health Statistics, 1992). Over the past 15 years, the death rate for diseases of the heart and blood vessels has declined dramatically. It has declined 35% for all cardiovascular diseases, 42% for coronary artery disease, and 54% for stroke deaths (Public Health Service, 1990). Among the reasons for this decline are not only changes in health behaviors, such as smoking reduction, lower fat diets, and more exercise, but also improvements in cardiac treatment so that more patients initially diagnosed with a heart attack or stroke survive the initial episodes.

Cancer is not one disease but a constellation of more than 100 different diseases, with the same underlying symptom—uncontrolled growth and spread of abnormal cells. The incidence rates (number of new cases) of all cancer sites combined among both men and women has been increasing over the past 15 years. Death rates from cancer have been declining, however, among all groups under 55 (Public Health Service, 1990). Lung cancer deaths are beginning to level off among men, probably due to gradual declines in the rates of smoking among white men. Unfortunately, lung cancer deaths are increasing among women, and will probably become the leading cause of cancer death in women in 1992, surpassing breast cancer ("Lung Cancer," 1992).

Currently, unintentional injuries are the fourth leading cause of death, with motor vehicle accidents accounting for half of those deaths. Other major causes of accidental injury death are falls, poisoning, drowning, and residential fires. Unlike heart disease, stroke, and cancer, unintentional injuries occur disproportionately among the young. In fact, injuries are the major cause of death in most of the age groups under 30. If one examines only deaths among people under 65, suicides and homicides (sometimes referred to as intentional injuries) are the fourth leading cause of loss of life. They are the leading cause of death among certain subgroups in the population, such as black male teenagers and those ages 21 to 30, leading to a linkage between violence as a public health issue and violence as a more general social policy concern. As recently as 20 years ago the areas of accidental and intentional injury were not always viewed as a part of health policy controversies within the United States, but beginning in the late 1970s, the attention to these two areas as important health problems began to increase.

Mortality figures are only one limited way to try to examine trends in health status. Other approaches examine not simply deaths, but illness (morbidity), disability, and life expectancy. Life expectancy is a time-specific concept. It refers to the age to which the average individual can be expected to live, given that the person has reached a specified age. The most commonly reported statistic, especially to compare health status across countries, is life expectancy at birth. In 1989 life expectancy at birth in the United States reached a record high of 75.3 years. This is more than 27 years longer than the average life expectancy at birth was in 1900. Thus average life expectancy has increased by almost 60% from the beginning of this century to 1987, largely due to the advances of science and public health in conquering life-threatening communicable diseases. Even over the past few years, life expectancy has been increasing, having improved more than a full year between 1980 and 1986 (Year 2000, Pepper Commission, 1990). Despite the improvements in this measure of health status, many countries outrank the United States based on this statistic. International rankings of life expectancy in 1986 indicated that males in the United States ranked 18th and U.S. females ranked 12th among all nations. Japan was the top-ranking country for both men and women, with a gap of 4 years for men between life expectancy in Japan and the United States, and a gap of 3 years for women (Public Health Service, 1990).

The previous chapter has already discussed some of the figures about infant mortality differentials between the United States and other countries, and has indicated that infant mortality is traditionally considered one of the best overall indicators of not only a nation's health but also its commitment to ensuring the health of its people. Over the past two decades, the U.S. infant mortality rate has improved steadily, from a figure close to 20 deaths per 1,000 live births in 1970 to 10.4 deaths per 1,000 live births in 1986, the lowest figure ever recorded in the United States. In contrast, in 1950 the rate was 29.2 deaths per 1,000 live births. Health experts generally agree that much of the improvement in life expectancy since the beginning of the century is due to reductions in the rate of deaths in the early years of life. This includes reduced numbers of deaths in the first year of life, as reflected in infant mortality statistics and reductions in childhood mortality from childhood illnesses, such as whooping cough, mumps, and measles, as well as other problems that used to plague children in the early years of life.

Trends and Differentials in Health Status
for Special Population Groups

The trends in disease patterns just reviewed relate to the general population. For some specialized populations, however, trends and current health status vary. This variation in health status based on income and racial/ethnic status creates one of the major controversies in health policy formulation in the United States today.

People with low incomes are one specialized population group of policy interest. Nearly one out of every eight Americans lives with an income below the federal poverty level. For children, these rates are even higher. About one-quarter of children under 6 are members of such families. In most countries and at most periods of time, there have been some differentials in health between rich and poor. Partially, describing a family as low-income is a shorthand that groups together individuals who are currently unemployed, have poorly paid jobs, have only a single mother caring for young children, or have a former major wage earner in the family who now can no longer work due to a serious illness. This last situation is one reason that some experts discuss the circularity of relating income and health, arguing that poor health can lower income, as well as the situation in which lowered income hinders access to food, health care, and housing and thus hinders health. This can occur, and it is very difficult to disentangle these effects. It is at least useful, however, to review statistics on current linkages between income levels and health status.

For almost all of the major chronic diseases, low income is a special risk factor. Risk of death from heart disease is 25% higher among low-income people than in the overall population; the incidence of cancer in a number of sites (but not all) is also higher among low-income groups, and survival rates are lower. Many types of injury rates are higher. Most clearly for indicators of child health, infant mortality rates are higher, iron deficiency in children is twice as common, as are high levels of lead in the blood. Poor children experience over twice the number of disability days as do children from families earning $25,000 a year or more (Public Health Service, 1990).

African-Americans are 12% of the U.S. population and make up one of the nation's largest minority groups. They are three times as likely to be poor as the white population. Life expectancy for blacks has actually fallen slightly in the 1980s, thus increasing the gap between whites and blacks. Interestingly, the leading causes of death are similar in the two groups. Black men are twice as likely to die from stroke as white men, and have a higher risk of cancer. Diabetes is more common among blacks. Blacks have almost double the rate of infant deaths throughout the first year of life. The homicide rate for black men between 25 and 34 is seven times that of whites. AIDS rates among blacks are triple that of whites (Public Health Service, 1990).

The second-largest and most rapidly growing minority group in the United States is Hispanics (Mexican-Americans, Puerto Ricans, Cuban-Americans, Central and South Americans, and others). Mexican-Americans represent two-thirds of the total in numbers. It is difficult to generalize across all Hispanics, because there is variability within the group on health risk and outcomes. Two factors stand out: the relative youth of this population group and its high birth rate. Hispanics have lower death rates than the general population for heart disease and cancer, but higher rates of unintentional injuries, homicide, liver diseases, cirrhosis, and AIDS. The high growth rate of this population makes it a group of special policy interest in the coming years.

Does Medical Care Equal Better Health?

Returning to general population figures, what is the explanation for overall improvements in life expectancy and reductions in infant mortality? Given the focus of much current health policy on the provision of health care services, what is the linkage between medical care and better health over time in the United States? Much of the thrust of health policy in the 1950s and 1960s emphasized the provision of more health care services, based on the assumption that more medical care equals better health. Increasingly, experts have pointed out that many of the factors that lead to good or bad health are not now and were not necessarily ever part of the traditional health care system.

McKinlay and McKinlay (1977) explore this question through the use of historical disease trend data in the United States. They argue that the introduction of specific medical measures and/or the expansion of medical services are generally not responsible for most of the modern decline in mortality. McKeown has provided a similar type of analysis for the decline of mortality in England and Wales during the eighteenth through the twentieth centuries (McKeown & Record, 1955, 1962; McKeown, Record, & Turner, 1975). In the eighteenth century, he concludes, the decline in mortality was largely attributable to improvements in the environment. For the second half of the nineteenth century, he argues, a reduction of deaths from infectious diseases explains the decline. He specifically calls into question the role of medical therapy in the mortality reductions.

In their major research article, the McKinlays (1977) provide data on the effect of medical interventions on the decline in the age- and sex-adjusted death rates of 10 common infectious diseases in the United States from 1900 through 1973. For example, for measles, they examine the change in death rates and plot the time point of the introduction of the vaccine in 1963. They conduct a similar analysis for each of the other diseases: tuberculosis, scarlet fever, influenza, pneumonia, diphtheria, whooping cough, smallpox, typhoid, and poliomyelitis. One of their most important conclusions is that only reductions in tuberculosis and pneumonia contributed substantially to the decline in total mortality from 1900 to 1973 (about 16.5% and 11.7%). The second is that only influenza, whooping cough, and poliomyelitis show substantial declines of 25% or more in mortality after the date of medical intervention. Thus they conclude that medical measures contributed little to the overall decline in mortality in the United States from 1900 to 1973.

Wildavsky (1977) has discussed the fallacy of the great equation that medical care equals health. One explanation of the fallacy is the "Paradox of Time." For this paradox, past successes lead to future failures. As the statistics we have just reviewed demonstrate, life expectancy has increased. Thus diseases that formerly led to death now lead instead to disability. The health care system is increasingly faced with an older population with more disabilities. With this aging population, cure becomes harder (as well as costlier) to achieve. As Wildavsky summarizes, "Yesterday's victims of tuberculosis are today's geriatric cases. The Paradox of Time is that success lies in the past and (possibly) the future, but never the present."

The other explanation that Wildavsky presents for the fallacy of the great equation is the concept of goal replacement. He argues that there has been displacement from health objectives to other social objectives, particularly within the United States. An example is a movement from an initial emphasis on health care in general to an increased emphasis on access to health care. This has resulted in the United States in an emphasis on more and better technology. Now the provision of the maximal level of service and technology has become the standard of care in many circles.

Both these provocative theses raise questions about prevention, as applied at both an individual and a societal level. Russell (1986) has recently raised a related question about the importance of individual preventive efforts and how those compare to cures and health care. Russell demonstrates that while many preventive measures do improve health, they are generally not without risk or cost and rarely reduce medical expenditures. These controversies also lead us to consider the idea of a continuum of health care policy intervention.

A Continuum of Health Care Policy Intervention

There are several ways of conceiving of a continuum of health policy intervention. One approach focuses on the society as a group and has traditionally focused on measures that relate less to individuals and more to the total group. These are the classical public health measures that both McKeown and McKinlay and McKinlay argue were important in mortality reductions in the United States and Great Britain in the past. Standard examples of such approaches include improved sanitation and sanitary engineering; attention to proper disposal of waste products, such that fecal material does not contaminate water supplies; attention to purity and cleanliness of milk, water, and foodstuffs; and attention to basic standards of living, such as not having people dwelling in overcrowded situations. From these, one can begin to talk of provision of adequate nutrition, heat in dwelling units, and other basic aspects of safety and welfare that begin to move to an individual level of analysis.

One way of conceiving of health policy for individuals is as intervention along a continuum of care ranging from a policy to keep people healthy to a policy to help the terminally ill die as gracefully and painlessly as possible. A way to simplify this continuum is to conceptualize three points: preventing illness for healthy people, maintaining and restoring health for ill people who can be returned to normal functioning, and preserving life as fully and meaningfully as possible for those who cannot be returned to normal functioning (Kronenfeld & Whicker, 1984).

What are some of the factors that affect individual health? One approach that has become the basis for much public policy directly in Canada, but to a large extent also in the United States, has been the LaLonde (1975) four sphere approach. LaLonde categories the four spheres that affect health as: (a) human biology, including genetic components; (b) the external environment, including the elements within it; (c) life-style—the customs and habits of living; and (d) health promoting and restoring systems of society, including environmental controls and regulatory measures, and preventive and medical treatment service of the health care system.

Generally, two or more of the four spheres interact to determine the overall condition of individual health. Clearly, for certain diseases, such as Tay-Sachs, genetics dominates; while for cirrhosis of the liver and lung cancer, life-style factors of drinking and smoking dominate and the importance of genetic factors is still debated. For some of the leading killers, such as heart disease and stroke, at least two and maybe three spheres are very important. High blood pressure and family history are part of human biology, with smoking, exercise, and diet are part of life-style factors. Many believe stressful working or other conditions also play an important role, and thus would include environment as playing a major role. For accidental injuries, external environment and life-style are quite important, and health promoting and restoring systems would impact upon the extent of injuries and their consequences, although not on their occurrence rates.

This general approach of examining the major risk factors for health, the synergism between them, and the issue of controllability of many of these risks was first explicitly raised as a health policy approach for the United States to consider with the publication of *Healthy People* (Public Health Service, 1979), the Surgeon General's report on health promotion and disease prevention. This report brought up the idea of the creation of a second public health revolution, the first being the struggle against infectious diseases of the late nineteenth century and twentieth century, which was so successful in improving life expectancy and health status. This report discussed a group of major risk categories very similar to the LaLonde approach and reported a consensus among health science researchers and the health community that the nation's health strategy needed to be dramatically recast to emphasize the prevention of disease. The report established broad national goals—expressed as reductions in overall death rates or days of disability—for the improvement of health of Americans at five major life stages: infants, children, adolescents and young adults, adults, and older adults. Further documents (Public Health Service, 1979) were based on a year-long series of meetings and papers involving more than 500 individuals and organizations from both the private and governmental health sectors, as well as university researchers. These goals became known as the 1990 objectives and became a major focus of health policy during the 1908s, especially public health related policy. About 225 specific objectives were listed. Certain important health problems, such as AIDS and Alzheimer's disease, were not included in these objectives, a criticism that has been noted and corrected in the new Year 2000 objectives (Andersen & Mullner, 1990). A general summary was that while many of the 1990s objectives were met (in high blood pressure control, smoking reduction, and dental health, for example), other areas met few objectives (pregnancy and infant health, nutrition, fitness, and violent behavior), and these areas remain important sources of controversy in health for the next 10 years (Andersen & Mullner, 1990).

Year 2000 Health Promotion and Disease Prevention Objectives: How Do We Move Beyond Goal Setting?

In 1987 a new process was begun to plan health objectives for the year 2000. In September 1988 work groups were organized by the Public Health Service (PHS) (part of the U.S. Department of Health and Human Services) and began to develop new goals and objectives, partially based on the 1990 objectives and the extent to which those had been achieved. More than 200 national membership organizations and all state and territorial health departments joined the PHS in a national consortium in support of the development of the Year 2000 objectives. As part of the process, it was emphasized that the new objectives should be realistic, be understandable to a broad audience, include outcomes and methods to achieve them, and be measurable (quantifiable). A series of hearings was held across the country, and draft copies of the objectives were circulated for comment by health professionals. The result of this process has become the most important emphasis in terms of health status and policy efforts for the next decade. The initial 21 priority areas were expanded to 22 priority areas, most of which are grouped into three broad categories of health promotion, health protection, and preventive services (Public Health Service, 1990).

Most public health experts now believe that this goal setting exercise has the potential for making major strides in improving health in the United States in the next decade. It has created a similar set of goals for official state and local health departments and for federal groups, such as the National Institutes of Health (NIH), that support much of the health-related research in the United States. One limitation may be funds, however, since funds for health education and promotion have often been those most subject to cuts in times of economic problems.

Three major overarching goals have been set. The *first* is to increase the span of healthy life for Americans. This means not only increasing the average life expectancy, but also setting a new measure that takes into account the average amount of time spent in a dysfunctional state due to either chronic or acute limitation. One major measure of dysfunction is limitation of major activities due to chronic conditions. The *second* goal is reducing health disparities among Americans. The emphasis within this overall goal is to close the gap between minorities and the white population in average life expectancy, in infant mortality rates, and in premature death both due to chronic illness and due to violence. The *third* major goal is to achieve access to preventive services for all Americans. This would include early and regular prenatal care for all pregnant women, appropriate child and adult immunization rates, and access to screening services.

While this chapter cannot review all of the objectives in any one of these areas, it will highlight a few as examples. Within the health promotion area, there are specific objectives in eight areas: physical activity and fitness; nutrition; tobacco; alcohol and drugs; family planning; mental health and mental disorders; violent and abusive behavior; and educational and community-based programs. In the physical activity areas, examples of objectives include reducing coronary heart disease deaths and increasing the proportion of people who engage in regular light to moderate physical activity for at least 30 minutes a day. Dietary objectives include reductions in dietary fat intake. A major tobacco objective is to reduce cigarette smoking to a prevalence of no more than 15% among people age 20 and older.

Health protection objectives focus on areas of unintentional injuries, occupational safety and health, environmental health, food and drug safety, and oral health. Examples of specific injury objectives include increasing use of such devices as bike helmets among children. Occupational safety and health objectives include improving standards to prevent major occupational diseases. Environmental objectives include such goals as reducing exposure to disease through air pollution, radon contamination, and toxic substance release.

Preventive services objectives include 15 to 20 specific objectives in each major area such as maternal and infant health; heart disease and stroke; cancer; diabetes and chronic disabling conditions; HIV infection; sexually transmitted diseases; immunization and infectious diseases; and clinical preventive services. An example of objectives from the maternal and child health area is to reduce the overall U.S. infant

mortality rate by the year 2000 to no more than 7 per 1,000 live births
and to reduce the black rate to 11. For cancer, goals are to reduce the
overall death rate to no more than 130 per 100,000 people.

It is important to appreciate the impact that accomplishment of the
Year 2000 objectives would have on overall health status in the United
States. A recent study estimated that the demographic impact of meeting
just the mortality targets set in the objectives would be an increase in
life expectancy of 1.5 to 2.1 years. Meeting the reductions in activity
limitations would result in an additional 2.5 to 2.9 years of limitation-
free life at birth (Stoto & Durch, 1991). Thus a major controversy in
overall health policy is the extent to which resources should be mar-
shaled toward the attainment of these objectives. In contrast, another
emphasis is provision of all types of health services to those without
such access, the other major policy issue in health. While these two
broad goals are not necessarily antithetical to each other, in the current
economic and political climate of limited resources, both the amount to
expend on health in total and how to distribute those funds are complicated and controversial issues.

AIDS as a Special Policy Concern

One special area relating to health status that has become very
controversial in the past 10 years is AIDS and HIV infection. This area
was not even included in the 1990 health objectives for the nation. The
first cases were reported in Los Angeles in 1981. By 1989 more than
115,000 cases of AIDS had been reported in the United States, and it is
projected that by 1993 there will be more than 400,000 cases and more
than 300,000 people will have died from the disease in the United States
(Public Health Service, 1990). In the 1989 death statistics, AIDS deaths
rose by one-third over the previous year to become the nation's 11th-
leading cause of death overall. It is the 7th-leading cause of years of
potential life lost before age 65. It is estimated that one major factor in
the increasing gap in life expectancies between blacks and whites is
AIDS. Death rates actually increased for the age group between 25 and
44 years of age, mostly because of the increase within this age span of
AIDS deaths (National Center for Health Statistics, 1992). AIDS is now
the leading cause of death for intravenous (IV) drug users in the United
States. Of all AIDS deaths, 64% are white males, 25% are black males,
and 6% and 4% are black females and white females, respectively.
Taking account of the smaller numbers of black males in the total popula-

tion, however, age-specific death rates are highest for black males. There is currently no known cure for AIDS.

What are the major risk factors for AIDS, and what does the near-term future (to the year 2000) hold for control of AIDS in the U.S. population? The public perception of AIDS in the United States began as a homosexual disease that predominantly struck young, white, gay men. Over time, the most commonly reported risk factors for AIDS have been changing. In a recent study of HIV positive blood donors in New York City, the most commonly reported risk factor for AIDS was still sexual contact with another man, followed by a connection with IV drug users or sex with an IV drug user (Cleary, Devanter, Rogers, Singer, Avorn, & Pindyck, 1991). The profile of the typical AIDS patient is changing from a gay, white man to a minority IV drug user. The number and proportion of AIDS cases associated with heterosexual transmission of the disease are increasing. Factors associated with increased risk of heterosexual transmission include multiple sex partners, the presence of other sexually transmitted diseases, and unprotected sexual contact with partners at higher risk of HIV infection ("The second 100,000 cases," 1992). The number of infected women and babies is also increasing. Moreover, most health experts believe the numbers currently seen are merely the visible tip of a largely submerged iceberg representing all HIV infection. The diagnosis of AIDS applies only to individuals affected by the human immunodeficiency virus (HIV) who also present with a variety of specific diseases rare among persons with healthy immune systems. The size of the submerged portion of the iceberg is most difficult to estimate, predominantly because those infected with HIV are asymptomatic or have few clinical complications for 7 to 10 or more years after first being infected (Ball & Turner, 1991).

Table 2.2 shows the number of AIDS cases reported by various patient characteristics from 1981 to 1990. These figures illustrate that AIDS at this time is still overwhelmingly a disease of males, with important concentrations in minority communities. Moreover, the disease is concentrated in states such as New York and California, although it is spreading to other states.

What is the impact of AIDS on the health care system, and what are the future prospects? As Table 2.3 illustrates, the number of patients discharged from hospitals for AIDS increased seven-fold over a 4-year period from 1984 to 1988. The number of days of care increased even more. Moreover, this impact is concentrated in certain states. In one study, hospitals in New York and California reported 37% and 20%,

Table 2.2 AIDS Cases Reported, by Patient Characteristics: 1981 to 1990 (Provisional: For cases reported in the year shown.)

Characteristic	Total	Number of Cases									Percent	
		1981-1982	1983	1984	1985	1986	1987	1988	1989	1990[1]	1981-1982	1990[1]
Total	142,424	838	2,059	4,435	8,182	13,124	21,117	30,858	33,714	28,097	100.0	100.0
Age:												
Under 5 years	1,937	12	31	47	110	156	265	443	503	370	1.4	1.3
5 to 12 years	442	1	1	3	18	28	56	126	102	107	0.1	0.4
13 to 29 years	29,144	196	457	960	1,685	2,815	4,385	6,383	6,780	5,483	23.4	19.5
30 to 39 years	65,581	396	929	2,108	3,838	6,093	9,634	14,199	15,553	12,831	47.3	45.7
40 to 49 years	30,726	169	446	923	1,707	2,685	4,516	6,529	7,340	6,411	20.2	22.8
50 to 59 years	10,330	58	166	312	626	968	1,553	2,163	2,431	2,053	6.9	7.3
60 years and over	4,264	6	29	82	198	379	708	1,015	1,005	842	0.7	3.0
Sex:												
Male	128,243	780	1,902	4,142	7,597	12,068	19,290	27,562	30,053	24,849	93.1	88.4
Female	14,173	58	157	293	585	1,056	1,826	3,294	3,658	3,246	6.9	11.6
Not reported	8	—	—	—	—	—	1	2	3	2	—	(Z)
Race/ethnic												
White, non-Hispanic	81,081	467	1,174	2,689	4,957	7,822	12,969	17,177	18,632	15,194	55.8	54.1
Black, non-Hispanic	41,119	251	565	1,119	2,080	3,392	5,382	9,107	10,321	8,902	30.0	31.7
Hispanic	18,785	117	311	605	1,085	1,785	2,554	4,274	4,352	3,702	14.0	13.2
Other/unknown	1,439	3	9	22	60	125	212	300	409	299	0.2	1.1

Leading States:[2]											
New York	32,178	1,456	865	1,584	2,483	3,781	3,966	6,975	6,022	6,046	54.4	21.5
California	27,653	120	440	1,002	1,936	2,615	4,853	5,743	6,435	4,509	14.3	16.1
Florida	12,684	69	153	314	554	1,024	1,662	2,696	3,492	2,720	8.2	9.7
Texas	10,424	20	89	250	433	940	1,670	2,231	2,399	2,342	2.4	8.3
New Jersey	9,638	63	136	281	468	767	1,509	2,455	2,231	1,728	7.5	6.2
Illinois	4,298	18	39	100	138	347	629	993	1,139	845	2.2	3.0
Pennsylvania	4,086	19	37	91	202	310	657	852	1,075	843	2.3	3.0
Georgia	3,816	13	25	56	191	304	517	839	1,102	769	1.6	2.7
Massachusetts	3,062	13	34	87	165	281	452	711	756	563	1.6	2.0
Maryland	2,785	5	27	54	148	188	457	545	719	642	0.6	2.3
District of Columbia	2,493	3	19	90	178	226	466	501	498	512	0.4	1.8
Ohio	2,121	8	7	30	53	212	335	507	485	484	1.0	1.7
Louisiana	2,069	—	18	55	104	165	337	401	513	476	—	1.7
Washington	1,958	1	6	59	112	170	328	349	497	436	0.1	1.6
Virginia	1,859	—	27	40	108	160	242	348	392	542	—	1.9
Michigan	1,795	4	9	32	51	150	211	456	505	367	0.5	1.3
Connecticut	1,733	10	18	57	86	176	251	415	432	288	1.2	1.0
Missouri	1,624	1	7	27	50	74	238	411	441	375	0.1	1.3
North Carolina	1,512	—	9	15	56	81	210	278	447	406	—	1.4
Colorado	1,451	5	21	38	52	166	226	325	389	219	0.6	0.8
Percent of total	90.7	98.8	96.5	96.1	94.1	92.5	91.0	90.8	88.9	89.4	(X)	(X)

— Represents zero. X Not applicable. Z Rounds to zero. [1]January 1 through August. [2]States with at least 1,400 total cases reported through August 1990.
SOURCE: U.S. Centers for Disease Control, Atlanta, GA, and Statistical Abstract of the U.S., 1991.

Table 2.3 Selected Measures of Hospital Utilization for Patients Discharged
With AIDS: 1984 to 1988

Measure of Utilization	Unit	1984	1985	1986	1987	1988[1]
Number of patients discharged	1,000	10	23	37	50	71
Rate of patient discharges[2]	Rate	0.4	1.0	1.6	2.1	2.9
Number of days of care	1,000	123	387	606	783	983
Rate of days of care[2]	Rate	5.2	16.3	25.3	32.4	40.3
Average length of stay	Days	12.1	17.1	16.2	15.7	13.8

[1]Comparisons of 1988 data with data for earlier years should be made with caution as estimates of change
may reflect improvements in the 1988 design rather than true changes in hospital use.
[2]Per 10,000 population. Based on Bureau of the Census estimated civilian population as of July 1.
SOURCE: National Center for Health Statistics, *Health, United States, 1989*, and *Statistical Abstract
of the U.S., 1991*.

respectively, of U.S. AIDS discharges (Ball & Turner, 1991). These
states have borne a disproportionate share of the cost burden of caring
for AIDS to this point. Eighty percent of all hospitals treating AIDS
patients are located in urban areas and they treat more than 98% of the
AIDS cases. Annual costs of AIDS are projected to climb as high as $5
to $13 billion a year by 1995 to the year 2000 (Public Health Service,
1990).

What can be done about AIDS? Major objectives in the Year 2000
document were to confine the annual incidence, increase the proportion
of sexually active unmarried people who use condoms to 50% (estimated in 1988 to be only 19%), and reduce the proportion of adolescents
who engage in sexual intercourse. Few issues in health have generated
the public controversies of AIDS, perhaps because of its connection
with sexual behavior, illegal behavior such as IV drug use, and the rapid
organization of AIDS patients into politically active pressure groups to
achieve greater funding for research into both a cure and treatment. It
appears that early successes in behavior changes among gay men are
not being duplicated among youths and drug users. In a time of limited
resources, there is a potential for conflict between those advocating
more treatment funds versus the need for preventive work with youths
and drug users. No easy solutions for this new disease are on the
horizon.

While the public views AIDS as very serious (more than 82% in a
recent survey) and most see it as becoming worse in the next 3 years
(71%), in public opinion surveys asking Americans to list the nation's

most important health problems, AIDS has never been listed by more than 5% of the population and has never been ranked among the top five problems (Blendon, Donelan, & Knox, 1992). Partially, this is because most Americans do not view themselves or the people they care most about as personally at high risk for AIDS. This is true even though increasing numbers of people have had personal contact with someone with AIDS. Estimates are that between one in five and one in six Americans knows someone with HIV disease. Given these mixed beliefs about personal risk and susceptibility, support for more funds for AIDS prevention, treatment, and research is mixed. While 60% of Americans in a recent survey did not believe that the government was doing enough about AIDS, the numbers favoring increased governmental spending for AIDS declined from 9 out of 10 in 1987 to 7 out of 10 in 1990 (Blendon et al.). These figures indicate the extent to which AIDS will probably remain one of the most controversial topics in health policy in the next decade.

3

Mental Health Concerns
and Behavioral Health

One common joke and complaint in the health care field is that researchers and caregivers separate the body and the mind. In many ways, this continues to be true. The care delivery system that has evolved to care for mental and behavioral problems has traditionally been different and very separate from the physical health care system. Many health insurance policies either totally exclude mental health coverage or have completely different limits and rules about such care. Moreover, the people who provide the services are different. The physicians who specialize in the mind and in related health problems are a separate specialty (psychiatrists) and there are whole special categories of caregivers in the mental health field (psychologists, psychiatric social workers). Policy concerns in the area have also been different, and most of the major legislation relating to these problems has been drafted and passed at a different point in time and often with little consideration of broader health issues. It might be argued that by presenting a separate chapter on these concerns, this book is also contributing to that separation. But at least we are going to review some of the issues in mental health and behavioral health.

Estimates of the range and the extent of mental illness vary a great deal, partially depending upon definitions. An estimated 23 to 29 million adults living in the community in the United States are severely incapacitated from mental disorders, excluding those related to substance abuse, a term which includes problems with both alcohol and drugs. Almost twice that number have experienced at least one diagnosable disorder at some point in their lives (Regier, Boyd, Burke, Rae, Myers, Kramer, Robbins, George, Karno, & Locke, 1988). One report estimated that in any given 6-month period, between 16% and 23% of the population has a diagnosable mental disorder (Richardson, 1988). A recent government report estimated that mental disorders cost the American public $73 billion annually, with about half of those costs reflecting lost productivity (House Committee on Governmental Operations, 1988). Suicide is the most serious potential outcome of mental disorder, and leads to about 30,000 Americans taking their own lives each year. Five thousand of these suicides occur under the age of 25. Additional costs of mental illness are the amount of lost work time and the disability related to the conditions. It is estimated that the number of bed days associated with depression is comparable to or greater than that associated with eight major chronic medical conditions (Wells, Stewart, & Hays, 1989).

A term increasingly in use today refers to *behavioral health*, including not only traditional mental health issues but also problems in dealing with alcohol and drugs. Alcohol and drug use is a major public health problem in the United States today, and one about which there is enormous controversy over the appropriate types of public policies. The idea of alcoholism as a disease was first proposed in the 1930s and did begin to increase the awareness of health problems related to excessive drinking. More recently, those working with alcohol have proposed the concepts of heavy drinking and problem drinking (Fingaratte, 1988). Costs of alcohol problems are estimated to be more than $70 billion per year (Public Health Service, 1990). While alcohol has often been considered merely a "social" substance, the "acceptable" drug in American society, the linkage between excessive alcohol consumption and health and safety problems is now well documented. Problems with alcohol and drugs both complicate and are a major factor in other public health problems, such as traffic accidents, murders, and the spread of AIDS. Alcohol has been linked to half of all deaths caused by motor vehicle accidents, as well as to fatal intentional injuries such as suicides and homicides. In addition, one-third of the victims in drowning and boating accidents are intoxicated (Perrine, Peck, & Fell, 1989). Also, alcohol use during pregnancy is the leading preventable cause of birth defects.

Both use of illegal drugs and addiction to such substances also cause a large array of social and health problems. Due to the illegal nature of the substances used, drug abuse has more commonly been considered a social and criminal justice problem rather than a health problem in the past. However, the linkage of drug abuse to being at risk for AIDS has focused greater attention on drug abuse as a health problem, as has the process described in the last chapter of the creation of health promotion and disease prevention objectives for the nation. Certainly, whether considered a general problem of social control, of the criminal justice system, or of the health care system, policies about the control of drug use are a major controversy currently. This chapter will discuss some of these issues, focusing partially upon the objectives for the year 2000 concerning goals related to use of alcohol and other drugs (Public Health Service, 1990). In addition, the mere presence of high rates of drug use has led to increased rates of other serious health-related problems in the United States. Through the sharing of contaminated needles, intravenous drug users have become the most rapidly increasing group of people with AIDS. It is estimated that 70% of murders in the average large city are linked to drug abuse (Public Health Service, 1990).

History of Mental Health Treatment in the United States

The history of organized treatment of the mentally ill in this country dates to the beginning of the nineteenth century. At that time, there was a push to create state mental asylums to house the mentally ill. Different interpretations exist about the reasons for this push. One approach argues for an idealistic interpretation (Rothman, 1971). The rise of the asylum is viewed as the product of a specifically Jacksonian angst or fear about the stability of the social order, combined with a naive and uniquely American utopianism about the value of the asylum to deal with and help correct the problem. In contrast, others have pointed out that the creation of asylums was not a uniquely American effort, and the rise in the United States is tied into an emerging capitalistic set of market relationships that made it more important to identify the able-bodied, who would be forced to work, from those who were not able-bodied (Richardson, 1988; Scull, 1985).

Whatever the ultimate motives behind the creation of state mental institutions, there can be little debate about the fact that by the end of

World War II there were major problems with state mental institutions. Many of the facilities were old and in bad physical condition; some were also drastically overcrowded. In general during this time, the provision of mental health services and the setting of most mental health policy were state-level functions, and the institutions were maintained as part of a state-run mental health system. Mental institutions served as little more than holding places for chronic mentally ill patients who received little in the form of treatment while living in conditions which were horrible—overcrowded, understaffed institutions where patients were often physically restrained, ill-fed, and ill-clothed. The general public view of mental institutions by the end of World War II was that they were places to protect the public from "crazy" people. Mental illness was highly stigmatized, and state funding was very limited given the numbers of people involved (Richardson, 1988).

A number of changes occurred in mental health treatment in the 1950s, some as a direct outgrowth of World War II. Twelve percent of all the men screened for induction into the military in World War II were rejected for neuropsychiatric reasons. In addition, mental illness or mental deficiency accounted for 37% of all discharges from the military in World War II. These figures spurred the passage of the National Mental Health Act of 1946 (PL 79-487). This act created the National Institute of Mental Health. The purposes of this agency were not to provide mental health care or pay for mental health services (the provinces of the states), but to provide assistance to state mental authorities, stimulate research through grants, support training of personnel, and create a National Mental Health Advisory Panel. One approach of NIMH was to encourage states to explore different models of service delivery other than large state mental institutions (Weiss, 1990). Spurred in several states by scandals over the conditions found at state-run facilities, both experts and the public began to question the role of large mental institutions. During the 1950s and 1960s, various cycles of reform of the institutions occurred (Morrissey, Goldman, & Klerman, 1985).

Another factor leading to both change and questions about the existing models of provision of mental health services was the development of psychopharmacology in the 1950s. New drugs led to major breakthroughs in the treatment of patients, allowing many patients previously considered incurable to be treated on an outpatient basis (Richardson, 1988). This change in clinical possibilities combined with a slow shift in state funding. In 1946 less than half the states provided any funding for mental health, except for the large public hospitals. Just 5 years later, only three states had no programs of beds in general hospitals and outpatient facilities.

These trends resulted in a major shift in federal policy toward the mentally ill in 1963 with the passage of the Mental Retardation Facilities and Community Mental Health Centers Construction Act of 1964 (PL 88-164). This act provided construction monies for community mental health centers that were to serve designated catchment areas of 74,000 to 200,000 people. Centers were mandated to provide five basic services: inpatient, outpatient, emergency, day treatment, and consultation and education services.

**Current Patterns of Mental Health Care
and Deinstitutionalization**

There are currently more than 3,200 mental health organizations providing care in the United States. Reflecting the history of such treatment, 77% are state funded. One major difference from earlier periods is that more than three-quarters of the care now provided is outpatient care, as contrasted to 1955, when the same percentage was inpatient care (Richardson, 1988). Facilities to treat the mentally ill are still important, however, and Table 3.1 provides some details on the types of mental health facilities in the United States and average daily inpatient costs, as well as some figures on expenditures for inpatient and hospital-based ambulatory care.

A major care and policy shift that has occurred in mental health over the past 30 years, with increasing emphasis in the past 15, is *deinstitutionalization*. This term describes a policy consciously encouraged by NIMH, and such legislation as the community mental health centers movement, to change the major locus of care away from large inpatient facilities to outpatient care, community settings, and halfway houses and smaller types of residential facilities for those who require long-term completely supervised care.

Changes in the actual numbers of patients may help readers appreciate the magnitude of the change. In 1955, 560,000 persons were hospitalized in state and county mental health institutions, while the numbers had declined to only 125,000 in 1981 (Shadish, Lurigo, & Lewis, 1989). Most of this decline occurred between 1965 and 1975. Between 1970 and 1973, 13 mental hospitals closed in eight states, and almost all state facilities had a decline in patient numbers. In contrast, community mental

Table 3.1 Mental Health Facilities—Summary by Type of Facility: 1988

Type of facility	Number of facilities	Inpatient beds Total (1,000)	Rate[1]	Inpatients Total (1,000)	Rate[1]	Average daily inpatients (1,000)	Inpatient care episodes[2] (1,000)	Expenditures Total (mil. dol.)	Per capita[3] (dol.)	Patient care staff[4] (1,000)
Total	4,941	272.0	111.5	228.0	93.0	227.9	2,232.3	23,071	95	382.0
Mental hospitals:										
State and county	286	106.8	43.8	100.3	40.7	99.5	407.5	6,990	29	116.9
Private[5]	886	67.6	27.7	52.9	21.6	52.9	457.6	5,915	24	87.0
General hospitals[6]	1,486	48.5	19.9	34.9	14.3	36.0	914.0	3,617	15	61.8
Veterans Administration[7]	135	25.7	10.5	19.5	8.0	19.6	265.7	1,290	5	21.6
Freestanding psychiatric outpatient services[8]	757	(X)	(X)	(X)	(X)	(X)	(X)	668	3	11.1
Other[9]	1,388	23.4	9.6	20.4	8.4	19.9	187.5	4,591	19	83.6

X Not applicable. [1] Rate per 100,000 population. Based on Bureau of Census estimated civilian population as of July 1. [2] Inpatient care episodes defined as the number of residents in inpatient facilities at the beginning of the year plus the total additions to inpatient facilities during the year [3] Based on Bureau of the Census estimated civilian population as of July 1. [4] Full-time equivalent [5] Includes residential treatment centers for emotionally disturbed children [6] Non-federal hospitals with separate psychiatric services [7] Includes Veterans Administration (VA) neuropsychiatric hospitals, VA general hospitals with separate psychiatric settings, and VA freestanding psychiatric outpatient clinics [8] Includes mental health facilities which provide only psychiatric outpatient services [9] Includes other multiservices mental health facilities with two or more settings which are not elsewhere classified, as well as freestanding partial care facilities which provide only psychiatric partial care services. Number of facilities, expenditures, and staff data also include freestanding psychiatric partial care facilities. Facilities, beds and inpatients as of year end 1988; other data are for calendar year or fiscal year ending in a month other than December, since facilities are permitted to report on either a calendar or fiscal year basis. Excludes private psychiatric office practice and psychiatric service modes of all types in hospitals or outpatient clinics of federal agencies other than Veterans Administration. Excludes data from Puerto Rico, Virgin Islands, Guam, and other territories.
SOURCE: U.S. National Institute of Mental Health, *Statistical Note*, series and unpublished data

health center outpatient visits increased from 379,000 in 1955 to 4.6 million in 1975 (Shadish et al.). In addition to the factors described in the previous section, one other major factor led to declines in mental institution numbers starting in 1972. A major court decision (*Wyatt v. Stickney*, 1972) enumerated the rights guaranteed to institutionalized patients (Shadish et al.). Many of these rights would lead to higher provision costs, and some states considered it preferable to discharge patients rather than try to comply with improved standards of care.

Under the banner of community mental health, but also with the goal of reducing the amount of funds that states provide to mental health care, a number of states embarked upon programs of closure of many facilities and major (more than 50%, and in many cases more than 75%) reductions in the number of patients in facilities. Length of stay decreased dramatically as well, so that although in 1950 a person diagnosed as psychotic in a state hospital was likely to be a patient for an average of 20 years, by 1975 the average length of stay for the same type of patient had decreased to 9 months. By 1980 the average length of stay in state mental hospitals was slightly more than 6 months, and the bulk of inpatients were now being treated in general hospitals with an average length of stay of 11.6 days (Kiesler, 1982a, 1982b).

The Future of Deinstitutionalization and Other Policy Issues

How successful was the deinstitutionalization approach? Why did it occur? Was it really done to save money or because policymakers were committed to a different model of care? Not all the changes related to deinstitutionalization have been positive. Many state hospital residents were discharged without adequate preparation and to inappropriate community placements. There was lack of coordination with community mental health centers. Cutbacks in funding in states often led to inadequate follow-up of patients. As a result, institutions not specifically designed for mental health care, such as nursing homes and boarding homes, became the largest single location of mental health treatment; however, little actual treatment occurred in such facilities. Rather, custodial care of a different nature occurred, and since many of these institutions are for-profit facilities, some abusive, detrimental, and neglectful care occurred. Other patients fell through the cracks of the multiple systems and became part of a growing homeless population (Brown, 1985a).

Much of the policy of removing patients from state mental institutions has resulted in a shift of chronic patient care from the mental health system to other social service systems. Specifically, state budgets for inpatient mental health have declined, but Medicaid and Social Security Supplemental Security Income (SSI) have increased, so federal dollars are now more important in provision of care for these patients. There has also been a transfer of authority from public to private care, since many patients use these new social service benefits to pay for care in privately run boarding homes. In addition, authority has been transferred from state mental health departments to public health and public welfare departments. One negative aspect of these transfers is that even less attention is being paid to the psychiatric and psychological needs of the patients (Brown, 1985a). There has also been a large growth in privately provided (often in for-profit facilities) mental health care, especially for the middle class that has some insurance coverage for mental health care.

For which patients has this policy been a success? It has worked best for acutely ill patients who respond quickly to antipsychotic medications. Many of those patients are now living in their own homes and functioning at jobs, a great improvement from the situation in the 1950s. Many never experience any hospitalization, given the success of treatment of these problems with medication in the community setting.

In contrast, deinstitutionalization of the chronic mentally ill has caused problems and has created a continuing controversy on how best to provide care for these patients. As a group, these patients have more frequent symptom relapses, respond less well to medication in general, and have a large array of deficits—cognitive, social, economic, and often familial—that impede any return to normal social functioning (Shadish et al.). Most of the patients are still in some type of institutional care today, although it as likely to be a nursing home as a traditional mental health hospital. One recent estimate was that 30% of nursing home patients had a chronic mental disorder and another 57% had a chronic condition of senility (U.S. Dept. of Health, Education and Welfare, 1980). An estimated 400,000 more chronic mental patients live in board-and-care homes, many of which provide a minimal quality of life.

Should we reinstitutionalize some patients? Today, one of the major controversies in chronic mental health policy concerns whether to return some patients to institutional settings. The creation of homeless mentally ill patients and patients who spend their entire lives in a room the size of a cheap motel room, with little social interaction, has led to a sense of discouragement about the possibility of seriously denting the problems of the chronic mentally ill. Privatization of services and model programs have reported very few successes for the chronic mentally ill. Yet a large number of studies have documented that alternatives to hospitalization attain better results on most outcome criteria than does traditional hospital care (Mechanic & Rochefort, 1990). The call today is for greater coordination of resources, yet both economics and geopolitical considerations make this difficult. One recent review of service strategies for the chronic mentally ill concludes that the larger the population and area served, the more potential for fragmented bureaucratic performance, and thus, not surprisingly, small states geographically do best in provision of mental health services (Dill & Rochefort, 1989). Another review of current mental health policy calls for coordination and provision of services by comprehensive state government agencies as an attempt to eliminate the fragmentation and duplication of current practices (Brown, 1985b).

Two other approaches receiving discussion are case management and capitation. Case management is partially seen as a solution to lack of coordination, and usually involves a one-on-one relationship with a social worker who plans a coherent program of services (Mechanic, 1987). One controversy about this approach relates to cost. Others relate to the difficulty of maintaining one consistent case manager over a number of years. Thus many believe this approach to be unworkable for large numbers of patients. Capitation in mental health has been applied in two different ways. One approach is to mainstream the elderly into health maintenance organizations (HMOs) and another is to develop special mental health organizations (MHOs). Controversy over this approach centers on the need to share risks to achieve reasonable overall costs. The problem with this approach for the chronic mentally ill is that almost all chronically ill mental patients have high costs (Mechanic & Rochefort, 1990). This approach may require more planning and careful implementation than other policy solutions, an approach that is not a strength of the mental health care system in the United States.

Homelessness: Is It a Mental Health Policy Issue?

One linkage between mental health policy and some other social policy and human services issues is homelessness. Estimates of the numbers of homeless vary widely, ranging from 200,000 to more than 2 million. In no way is the homeless problem a simple outcome of changes in mental health policy, since many factors contributed to the rise of homelessness in the late 1970s and 1980s. However, it is also clear that one part of the homeless problem is linked to changes in mental health policy, specifically deinstitutionalization. The majority of the studies that try to estimate linkages between homelessness and mental health suggest that between one-quarter and one-half of the homeless have significant psychiatric problems (Institute of Medicine, 1988; Rossi, Wright, Fischer, & Willis, 1987). Not all of these people have a prior history of psychiatric hospitalization, however. The proportion of homeless acknowledging a history of psychiatric hospitalization ranges from 11% to 33% (Institute of Medicine, 1988; Mechanic & Rochefort, 1990; Roth, Bean, & Hyde, 1986). These estimates predominantly relate to serious mental illness such as schizophrenia, affective disorders, and mood disorders (Levine & Rog, 1990). In addition, some proportion of the homeless have problems with alcohol and drugs. Current estimates of problems with alcohol among the homeless range from 29% to 55%, with some arguing that the proportion of homeless with alcohol problems is actually down as the number of homeless, previously working poor families increases (Wright, 1989). Many more of the homeless exhibit peculiarities of life-style (such as saving of materials, carrying things in paper bags, rummaging through garbage cans, and not being physically clean), which lay people routinely mistake for mental illness but which also may be a coping reaction to current living situations.

One of the major controversies about homelessness revolves around the extent to which sending people out of state mental institutions "caused" the problem. In addition, the mentally ill homeless represent one of the types of homeless people most feared by others in society. These mentally ill homeless are viewed by much of the public as people who are unstable and could possibly become dangerous to others. Reports and newspaper articles in the popular press have presented figures contending that the rate of mental health problems among the homeless ranges as high as 90%. These figures are clearly exaggerations of the actual situation.

The largest mental health related problem for the homeless is that the much smaller proportion of the homeless with serious mental health problems is receiving little service from the mental health care system (Roth et al., 1986). One major policy change needed is for providing more mental health care services in forms likely to reach the homeless, such as street clinics and outreach facilities. More contact with mental health professionals could help to provide services (including more appropriate living situations) to some portion of the homeless. A related issue is the large number of physical health problems in the homeless population and the need to provide some care for these problems (Wright, 1989). Part of the controversy over homelessness and mental health is that short-term solutions will not resolve what has become a long-term problem. Long-term solutions will be expensive, however. The provision of services to this population, be they mental or physical health services, will require additional expenditures of state and federal tax dollars, a major issue at a time of economic problems. Many policy experts have argued that the homeless, regardless of whether they are mentally ill, are viewed as an important issue only when the numbers become so large as to intrude upon the comfortable existence of those better off. Thus solutions are not easy to effect nor do they generate a wide public consensus.

Drugs and Alcohol as a Health Policy Issue

A Confusing History

The history of alcohol and drug control in the United States is a twisted one, focusing at various times on very different strategies. Unquestionably, Americans drank far more alcohol, from early colonial days throughout the early nineteenth century, than we do nowadays. Attitudes changed sharply from 1800 to 1850, and per capita consumption fell from 5 gallons a year to 2.5, possibly due to the growth of a mercantile work ethic as well as changing notions of "diseases" (Fingarette, 1988). A temperance movement began with a single solution, Prohibition, and a belief that alcohol in any form could lead to habitual drunkenness. The somewhat simplistic notion of banning completely these substances became in the late 1800s the major policy approach to the control of alcohol (and in a somewhat different way, drugs) in the United States. In fact, the major legislation to make many drugs that are prescription drugs today (such as morphine and various forms of cocaine) controlled was only passed at the beginning of the twentieth century. Until then, many of these substances were widely available in over-the-counter patent medicines.

In 1919 the temperance movement achieved its major objective, the Eighteenth Amendment to the Constitution, banning the production, sale, and transportation of intoxicating liquors. Reviews of the impact of Prohibition have traditionally focused on the impossibility of enforcement and the growth in gangsterism related to the illegal importation and sale of alcohol in the 1920s. The law was repealed in 1933, and attitudes toward alcohol returned to an acceptance of social drinking. Not as often publicized, however, is that the cirrhosis death rate was reduced from 11.8 per 100,000 in 1916 to 7.2 in 1932, the year before Prohibition was ended. In contrast, the cirrhosis death rate in the United States climbed as high as 16 in 1973 (Knowles, 1977).

Modern Attempts to Control Alcohol Usage: Is It a Disease?

Despite the success of Prohibition in health terms, alcohol use became more socially acceptable after the end of Prohibition in the 1930s. Despite increasing attitudes of public acceptance of drinking, the United States has remained a culture of constraint as compared to some other countries in the world in which the drinking of some alcohol (such as wine with a meal by even the young) is a daily occurrence (Beauchamp, 1980).

The whole professional approach to alcoholism as a problem was modified in the 1930s and 1940s, both by alcohol researchers and in the treatment area. Alcoholics Anonymous (AA) was founded in 1935 and focuses on an approach to treatment that stresses that most people can drink socially, but some (probably for biological reasons) are unable to. For these people, abstinence is the only way. Additionally, the program emphasizes acknowledgement of a problem with alcohol and relation to a higher power (Fingaratte, 1988; Kronenfeld, 1988). The AA approach was buttressed by two landmark articles by Jellinek (1946, 1952), an early alcohol researcher, which described alcohol patterns similar to the model proposed by AA. The veracity of these articles has recently been challenged, since most of the data in them were obtained from interviews with male alcoholics already in AA.

Whether alcoholism is a disease and whether a disease approach is the best approach is still a matter of major controversy, with one group of genetic researchers trying to locate a gene for alcoholism (which would reinforce the disease concept), while others argue that it is a behavior disorder and calling it a disease reflects a tendency both in society and in health care to "medicalize" social problems (Fingaratte, 1988; Zola, 1990).

An Alternative Approach—The Public Health Model for Alcohol and Drug Control

Clearly, one policy approach toward alcohol problems that has been gaining acceptance is a public health view of alcohol. This approach sees community alcohol problems as the predictable and expected consequence of a "consumption ethic," which maintains maximum legal availability of alcohol as a consumer product (Beauchamp, 1980). Additionally, this ethic is related to widespread advertising that connects alcohol with affluence. Another aspect of this approach has been relatively low taxation rates on alcoholic beverages, leading to a pattern in the United States (unlike many other Western counties) of higher rates of alcohol consumption in lower social classes. As Beauchamp has summarized the new public health approach, it focuses on: (a) identifying and controlling hazards; (b) prevention by controlling exposure; and (c) the creation of a sense of public responsibility, leading to a policy of discouraging consumption and increasing taxation.

This "public health" orientation is reflected in the new Year 2000 major objectives and goals relating to drug and alcohol use. Three different types of goals are presented: those focusing on consumption and rates, those focusing on teenagers and education, and those focusing on legal and control issues.

The focus on health-related aspects of these questions, rather than legal and control issues, is increasingly accepted by much of the public. These include reducing the number of deaths by alcohol-related motor vehicle accidents from 9.8 per 1,000 in 1987 to 8.5, reducing cirrhosis of the liver deaths (which are largely attributable to heavy alcohol consumption), and reducing drug-related deaths and drug-abuse-related hospital emergency room visits.

There are also many objectives that relate to reducing risks, particularly in young people, and to changing legislation. Both of these sets of objectives relate to some of the major controversies today about how to deal with alcohol and drugs. There is much broader agreement that alcohol abuse should be viewed as a behavioral health problem and a difficulty in controlling one's behavior around an addictive substance. Conversely, there is far less agreement where the illegality of the substance creates debates on whether policy for the user should focus on punishment of criminals or on treatment of those with a health problem. However, viewing alcohol as a "public health problem" is a recent approach and one that the alcohol researchers and policymakers within the federal government have begun to support. Within the past decade such leaders have advocated for warning labels on alcoholic beverages, warning labels specifically relating to fetal alcohol syndrome, and changes in advertising practices. This has been a major policy change from the 1950s, '60s, and '70s and probably reflects broadened support among the public at large for examination of policy related to drinking.

The most broadly supported objectives are those relating to risk reduction among youth. Most policy experts and much of the general public agree in principle that young people should not experiment with tobacco, alcohol, and illegal drugs, and that school health education programs to spread these messages are appropriate. Year 2000 objectives include increasing by one year (from 13.1 years of age to 14.1 years of age) the average age of first use of alcohol; reducing to 29% the usage of alcohol in the past month, by those 18-20 years of age, from figures as high as 58% in 1988; and increasing the proportion of high school seniors who associate risk of physical or psychological harm with the heavy use of alcohol.

Much of the controversy in this area relates to the old "do what I say, not what I do" approach. While many parents and restaurants support such efforts in theory, in practice they allow their high school age children to drink at special parties or are less than rigorous in checking the age of clientele. Attitudes and practices are changing, however, with most college campuses now strictly enforcing rules about on-campus drinking that were honored only on paper in previous times.

The most controversial of the Year 2000 objectives focus on legislative and work changes. One recommendation is for adoption of alcohol and drug policies by 60% of work sites. While the majority of workers support control of alcohol and drugs at work, the use of mandatory urine tests to enforce such policies raises the specter of infringement on individual rights and is viewed negatively by many workers. In addition, tests for drugs are particularly sensitive to an array of other substances and drugs (including legal, prescribed ones), and many workers fear dismissal despite no inappropriate behavior. In times of high unemployment, workers may accept such requirements reluctantly.

The issue of raising taxes on alcoholic beverages is also controversial, as it results in a tax increase for those who do drink. Yet policymakers and the Year 2000 objectives view this as one of the most important ways to control teenage drinking, since younger drinkers are more sensitive to price increases. The federal tax on alcohol in beer and wine has remained constant since 1951 but was increased on alcohol in distilled spirits in 1985, after no change for 35 years. Moreover, the federal tax on beer, the drink of choice among youth, is less than one-third the tax on alcohol in distilled spirits. Also, alcohol taxation rates are much higher in Canada and most European countries. Yet rates of alcohol consumption are tied in with current profits of beer, wine, and alcohol producers, a major industry. Thus proposals to change these taxes arouse an organized and well-funded opposition within the industry.

Even more controversial with the public are changes in laws relating to alcohol and drinking. There is now a large social advocacy group, MADD (Mothers Against Drunk Driving), which is trying to have several of the Year 2000 goals enacted, including tightening driver's license suspension or revocation laws for those who drink and drive, and reducing the amount of blood alcohol concentration allowed legally. In regard to the reduction in allowed level of blood alcohol concentration, the legal limit in most states is now a blood alcohol concentration level of 0.10. The Year 2000 suggestion is a reduction to .94 for those 21 and over and no legally allowed level for those under 21. One suggestion for tougher enforcement is administrative driver's license suspension while awaiting trial for any person arrested for drunk driving. Though this idea has some appeal, because trials can move slowly and plea bargaining can reduce a penalty, these suggestions raise concerns about civil liberties and punishment of people prior to conviction. There is fear, fostered by opponents of change, that these actions would reduce certain fundamental rights long cherished in the United States. In addition, opponents of legal change raise the issue of many drivers not being able to work if they could not drive for a month following a possibly erroneous arrest. Again, many other countries have much tougher legislation about drinking while driving; however, those countries also have better public transportation systems, which allow for easier travel between home and work for those who might have lost their licenses because of drunk driving.

Thus major controversies exist on several fronts in regard to alcohol and drug policy. How strict should new laws be, and how acceptable to the public are increasingly strict laws on legal drinking levels and drinking and driving? How hypocritical is it for adults to impose tougher controls and increased restrictions on youth drinking if they do not curb their own behavior? Can former alcoholics learn to drink safely or is it a genetic, inherited problem? Is any drinking desirable and, if not, should advertising be banned and should taxation discourage such approaches?

For drugs, one entire area of controversy is whether to legalize some substances, and raise all of the concerns we now see in the alcohol area into that area, or whether to continue to keep all such drugs illegal. Given the relationship of AIDS to drug use, another issue is the extent to which we try to discourage the spread of AIDS, even if at some points it means condoning the use of drugs (Pincus, 1984). What are the messages we send as a society if we provide free needles and bleach to clean needles to prevent the spread of AIDS? Yet, if we do not adopt such policies, AIDS may spread more quickly and the sexual partners of IV drug users will become a growing source of increased AIDS infection. Easy answers are hard to come by in the area of alcohol and drug abuse, both because of the lack of a public consensus and because of the moral overtones of these issues, as contrasted with physical diseases.

4

Reproductive Health Concerns
and Abortion

One area of health-related policy that is a source of great controversy is reproductive health concerns, including access to birth
control, the development of new birth control technologies, and abortion. There is currently a major political struggle occurring in this
country about reproductive rights. Much of this struggle centers on
abortion, but there are spillovers into birth control technology and the
reaction to new reproductive technologies. These controversies are
linked with both health specific issues and gender specific issues relating to changing roles of women in society. In this area, perhaps more
clearly than in some other areas of health policy, the interrelationships
between broader social policy, political issues, and health care issues
are strong and easily apparent. The strong political overtones in this
area are partly new because the fervor of the arguments has gained
greatly in American society in the past 20 years. However, there have
always been political overtones and linkages between policy in the
reproductive health area and gender roles, because the issue of controlling reproduction and the ability to control family size is so inextricably
linked to the everyday life of most women and most men.

Some controversies about birth control relate to the slow development
and even slower dissemination of new technologies in the American

market; others center on issues about the availability of information to teenagers. These include the current controversy over teenage pregnancy, why it has been increasing, and the extent to which it is negative both for the young women who become pregnant and for society as a whole.

In the abortion area, there are several controversies, the most fundamental of which concerns whether there is a right to abortion and whether abortion should continue to be legal in the United States. If abortion remains legal, other controversies relate to the use of federal funding and the availability of abortions to the poor as well as the rich. A third controversy concerns the rights of health care providers: Should they be forced to learn how to perform abortions, and are many being prevented from learning these techniques currently because of the fervor of the pro-life movement?

Prior Policy on Birth Control and Its Use

The desire to control fertility and the number of births, particularly among women but also to a slightly lesser extent among men, is timeless. Going back to Egyptian, Greek, and Roman times, there are references to devices to control fertility and also of charms to induce fertility. Attempts to control births can be divided into two periods: traditional attempts to control births, in which technology was neither well developed nor very effective, and modern birth control, beginning in the late nineteenth century, in which more effective techniques were gradually developed and disseminated (Whicker & Kronenfeld, 1986). Modern birth control can also be divided into two technologies, that of barrier or restraint methods, and that of newer technologies, such as the pill, the IUD, and hormonal implants.

Barrier methods are among the earliest of birth control technologies. Condoms from animal skins became available in the eighteenth century, but were very expensive. Mass production of relatively cheap condoms from nonanimal sources did not occur until the vulcanization of rubber in 1843 and 1844. Once condoms became less expensive, their diffusion depended upon where they were sold. Initially they were available almost exclusively in pharmacies. By the 1920s condoms were carried in many other places, such as gas stations and small groceries, where contact was less personal.

The first modern female barrier contraceptives were the diaphragm and the cervical cap, introduced in the nineteenth century. Diaphragms became popular in Europe and England during the late nineteenth century. Recognition and use of these methods in the United States, however, lagged behind. By the 1920s middle-class women in the United States were using diaphragms. The birth control pill and the IUD first became commercially available in the United States in the 1960s.

The development of modern birth control technology does not necessarily imply social and legal availability. The dissemination of information about birth control was particularly restricted in the United States by the passage of the federal Comstock Law in 1873. It prohibited the dissemination of contraceptives and contraceptive information, closing the mails to this material. The restriction of contraceptive materials was strengthened in 1897 by the passage of another law prohibiting the deposit of contraceptive materials with a common carrier. As a result, magazine and journal editors of professional as well as general lay publications were afraid to publish articles on contraceptives. Anticontraceptive laws were rigorously enforced before the 1920s and sporadically enforced through the 1920s and early 1930s.

While public support for restrictive contraceptive laws was declining, there was insufficient political strength in favor of broader dissemination of birth control, and thus in many places the legal restrictions were not repealed. The restrictive laws continued to inhibit the spread of birth control information and devices, especially for the poor (Dienes, 1962). The Comstock Law remained in effect until 1936 and the crucial decision of *United States v. One Package* (Sulloway, 1959). Availability of information to the poor increased after this decision.

The right to practice birth control was established only recently under U.S. law. In 1965 *Griswold v. Connecticut* was the first constitutional precedent that the use of birth control was a right for married persons, not a crime. Not until 1972 were laws that prohibited the dispensing of contraceptives to unmarried persons, or by other than a physician or pharmacist, held to be unconstitutional, in *Eisenstadt v. Baird,* heard before the Supreme Court (Andersen, 1983).

With the wide availability of oral contraceptives and IUDs in the 1960s, the use of barrier methods decreased rapidly. In 1955 more than half the white married couples using contraception relied on barrier methods. By 1965 the proportion of contraceptive-using white married couples relying on the diaphragm had dropped to 10% as a result of the availability of the pill and IUDs; by 1976 that figure had declined

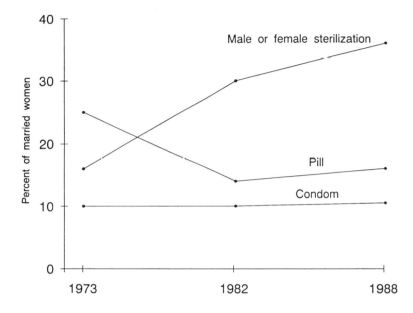

Figure 4.1. Percentage of Married Couples (wives 15-44 years of age) Using Sterilization, the Pill, and Condoms: United States, 1973, 1982, and 1988
SOURCE: *Advance Data,* National Center for Health Statistics, March 20, 1990.

further to 3%, despite the growing concern and publicity about the deleterious effects of the pill and IUDs (Mosher, 1981; Ryder & Westoff, 1971). The pill was the most commonly used form of contraception among all women and married couples by 1973. Retail prescriptions of oral contraceptives peaked at about 68 million in 1973. They have remained around 50 to 60 million since 1981 (Gerstman, Gross, Kennedy, Bennett, Tomita, & Stadel, 1991). After 1973 use of the pill declined, especially among married women, but it still remained the leading contraceptive method in both 1982 and 1988. By 1988, 31% of contracepting women were using the pill (Mosher & Pratt, 1990b). Because of problems with some forms of IUDs, their use declined from 7% in 1982 to only 2% in 1988.

The method that has been gaining in popularity over the 1980s is sterilization. Surgical sterilization has become the most popular method of contraception among married women, as shown in Figure 4.1.

In 1976, 26% of currently married women were using the pill, and 19% relied on sterilization of either themselves or their husbands. By 1982 sterilization was relied on by 27% of currently married women, and the pill was used by only 14% (NSFG, 1982). Combining both male and female sterilization, 39% of contracepting couples were using one of these two approaches in 1988 (Mosher & Pratt, 1990b). The percentage of married couples using sterilization as a method of contraception doubled in the 15 years from 1973 to 1988 (Mosher & Pratt, 1990a).

As Table 4.1 shows, sterilization as a form of birth control becomes more popular as women become older. Use of the pill drops off sharply when women become 35 or older. Condoms have become a more popular birth control choice of younger women over the decade of the 1980s, perhaps due to the spread of AIDS and the double role of condoms as protection against both unwanted pregnancies and transmission of AIDS.

This brief review of past legislation and availability and use of birth control in the United States should demonstrate that there has been some controversy over the availability of birth control in this country in the past. Today, more of the focus of controversy is on abortion and new fertility-related technologies, although there are some points of controversy about new types of birth control that will be reviewed in later sections.

Prior Policy About Abortion and Its Use

In the debate of the past 20 years, the heart of the abortion controversy has been framed as a conflict between a woman and the embryo within her (Sprague, 1991). Increasingly, much of the debate has focused upon the status of the fetus. This emphasis on the fetus is a relatively new addition to controversy about abortion. In early Greek and Roman times, restraints on abortion were intended to protect the pregnant woman from mutilation (Rodman, Sarvis, & Bonar, 1987). The desire to halt unwanted pregnancies is also discussed in writings from ancient societies, and charms and approaches to lead to miscarriages were often described, but frequently ineffective. Herbal and other abortifacients were in frequent use in Europe in the preindustrial period. Thus, abortion is an old technique, although not always a safe or efficacious technique.

The right to use abortion as a technique to control births has long been a controversial issue in U.S. society. Abortion was generally not forbidden during the colonial period, but laws restricting abortion

Table 4.1 Number of Women 15-44 Years of Age and Percent Distribution by Current Contraceptive Status and Method, According to Age: United States, 1982 and 1988. (Statistics are based on sample of the female population of the conterminous United States. Data for 1988 are preliminary.)

Contraceptive Status and Method	15-24 Years 1988	15-24 Years 1982	25-34 Years 1988	25-34 Years 1982	35-44 Years 1988	35-44 Years 1982
All women (number in thousands)	18,592	20,150	21,726	19,644	17,582	14,305
Percent distribution						
Total	100.0	100.0	100.0	100.0	100.0	100.0
Sterile	3.1	3.2	27.0	27.9	61.3	60.1
Surgically sterile	2.4	2.6	26.0	26.4	58.7	57.3
Contraceptively sterile	2.2	2.4	23.3	21.5	46.7	39.0
Female	1.6	1.3	16.6	14.8	32.5	26.8
Male	*0.6	1.1	6.7	6.7	14.2	12.2
Noncontraceptively sterile	*0.2	*0.2	2.7	4.9	12.0	18.3
Female	*0.2	0.2	2.7	4.6	11.9	17.4
Male	*0.0	*0.0	0.0	0.3	0.0	0.8
Nonsurgically sterile	0.7	*0.6	0.9	1.5	2.7	2.8
Pregnant or postpartum	5.0	6.3	7.6	6.5	1.1	1.0
Seeking pregnancy	2.7	3.5	5.8	6.2	2.4	2.5
Other nonuser[1]	45.7	48.6	16.7	14.2	13.5	13.8
Never had intercourse	30.0	32.5	3.6	2.7	1.6	2.0
No intercourse in last 3 months	5.4	6.9	6.4	5.1	6.8	5.8
Intercourse in last 3 months	7.8	9.2	6.4	6.5	5.0	6.0
Nonsurgical contraceptors	43.5	38.4	43.0	45.2	21.8	22.6
Pill	29.7	23.5	21.6	17.1	3.0	2.3
IUD	*0.1	1.4	1.4	6.5	2.1	4.2
Diaphragm	1.3	3.7	4.8	6.8	4.1	2.4
Condom	9.5	5.5	9.1	7.6	7.7	7.0
Foam	*0.1	0.8	0.8	1.5	0.8	1.8
Periodic abstinence[2] ·	*0.6	1.2	1.7	2.8	1.8	2.6
Natural family planning	*0.2	*0.1	0.5	0.6	0.4	0.3
Withdrawal	1.5	1.2	1.9	1.2	0.6	0.8
Douche	*0.0	*0.1	0.0	0.1	0.2	0.3
Other methods	*0.5	1.0	1.7	1.8	1.4	1.1

[1] Includes women who have had intercourse only once, not shown separately.
[2] Includes natural family planning and other types of periodic abstinence.
SOURCE: *Advance*, National Center for Health Statistics, March 20, 1990; and *National Survey of Family Growth*. Data for 1988 are preliminary. Data for 1982 are based on a revised classification of the contraceptive intent of sterilization operations, intended to be comparable to the 1988 classification.

became part of statutory law in the nineteenth century. For the next century, abortion was illegal in most circumstances in the United States. Even illegal abortion was heavily restricted to very wealthy women with unusual connections—or to backroom abortions of questionable safety and efficacy. In the 1960s two events generated enormous publicity about the lack of availability of abortions. The linkage of the drug thalidomide with serious birth defects and the taking of the drug by several prominent American women while in Europe generated support for making abortion available in the early 1960s, as did a German measles (rubella) epidemic that hit in 1964. Gradually, states began to reform their laws. With the exception of a few states with very liberal laws, the right of women to abortion was not established until the 1973 Supreme Court decisions of *Roe v. Wade* and *Doe v. Bolton*. The original decision argued that three rights collided: the constitutional right to privacy, the right of the states to protect maternal health, and the right of the state to protect developing life.

The Court set up different restrictions in the trimesters of pregnancy, arguing that in the first trimester the woman's right to decide her future privately took precedence. In the second trimester, while the state could not deny abortion, it could insist on reasonable standards of medical procedure to protect the health of the mother. In the third trimester, abortion could be performed to preserve the life or health of the mother (Goldstein, 1979). Safety has increased as a result of both the legalization of abortion and improved technologies. First and second trimester abortions were legalized in the United States as part of the 1973 Supreme Court decision. After that decision, deaths from illegal abortions in the United States declined from 39 in 1972, before national legalization, to 3 in 1976. The amount of controversy about abortion has increased greatly since 1980 and the raising of this issue to a position of increased political prominence by the Reagan administration. Despite this controversy, the number of abortions performed has remained relatively unchanged form 1980 to 1988 (Henshaw & Van Vort, 1990). The actual abortion rate among women ages 15 to 44 declined very slightly from 29 per 1,000 in 1980, to 28 in 1985, and 27 in 1988 (Henshaw & Van Vort, 1990).

Linkages of Birth Control to General Health Issues and Special Policy Concerns

There are a number of reasons why reproductive policy is such an important part of health care policy. Many aspects of the health of

Table 4.2 Percentage of High School Students[1] Reporting Contraceptive[2] Use at Last Sexual Intercourse, by Sex and Race/Ethnicity—United States, Youth Risk Behavior Survey, 1990[3]

Race/Ethnicity	Female		Male		Total	
	%	(95% CI[4])	%	(95% CI[4])	%	(95% CI[4])
White	81.1	(=2.7)	80.1	(=4.9)	80.6	(=3.1)
Black	71.4	(=6.7)	76.3	(=4.7)	74.3	(=4.3)
Hispanic	62.6	(=6.9)	69.1	(=5.9)	66.2	(=4.9)
Total	77.7	(=2.5)	77.8	(=3.7)	77.7	(=2.5)

[1] Among students reporting sexual intercourse during the 3 months preceding the survey.
[2] Contraceptive methods include birth control pills, condoms, withdrawal, or another method.
[3] Unweighted sample size – 11,631 students.
[4] Confidence interval
SOURCE: *MMWR*, vol. 40, January 3, 1992, p. 887.

women from 15 to 44 partially relate to issues of reproduction and control of fertility. While the Year 2000 objectives in this area are limited, due to the political controversies about the importance of birth control and the right to abortion, there are objectives relating to family planning and maternal and infant health.

One whole set of objectives relates to issues of teenage pregnancies and pregnancies in which the mother is not currently married. Teenage pregnancies linked to rising rates of teenage sexual activity are a serious problem. In addition to the social complications that may arise from a teenage pregnancy, such as retarding an adolescent's progress toward social and economic independence and progress in school, there is also evidence of poorer outcomes among teen mothers. One Year 2000 goal is to increase to at least 90% the proportion of sexually active, unmarried young people who use contraception (Public Health Service, 1990). As Table 4.2 shows, the current use rates among white teenagers are around 80%, with even lower figures for blacks (74% overall) and Hispanics (66%).

Another Year 2000 goal in this area is to reduce the proportion of all pregnancies that are unintended (both unwanted, such as did not want at all, and mistimed, such as occurring earlier than desired) to no more than 30% of all pregnancies by the year 2000. The lack of use of contraception by teenagers is an important explanation of why the rate of unintended pregnancies among young women in the United States is twice the rate in most European countries (Hilts, 1990). It is far more important than are differences in teenage initiation of sex, which appears to be similar across the various countries.

This issue of unwanted childbearing has important linkages to reproductive health policy and also health outcomes of infants. Clearly there is controversy about policies related to unwanted childbearing, but it is an important overall health issue, given linkages between unwanted childbearing and poor pregnancy outcomes, as well as child abuse as the child grows. About 12% of childbearing in the United States in 1988 was unwanted and another 27% was mistimed (Miller, 1992). The trend in these two figures is up about 29% since 1982. Rates are higher in certain population groups, such as teenagers, poor people, minorities, and the unmarried. The increase in these figures in the 1980s suggests that ground gained in the 1970s, which enabled women to limit their fertility, was lost in the 1980s (Miller, 1992). During that decade, there was a one-third reduction in public funding of contraceptive services and reduced access to abortion (Gold & Daley, 1991; Henshaw & Van Vort, 1990).

Major New Controversies Related to Reproductive Health Policy

There are three major areas of controversy currently related to reproductive health policy. The first area concerns policies relating to availability of birth control, including the question of the amount of research being done and the numbers of methods currently available. The second area relates to the development of new reproductive technologies, many of which deal with new methods of improving fertility. These include such developments as surrogate motherhood and test tube babies. The third area covers issues specifically relating to abortion. These areas are not independent, however, since much of the debate about new methods of birth control is linked to debates about abortion.

Birth Control Research and Methods

One major concern with birth control policy today is the limitation on the number of methods currently available. Some of the methods that were important in the past have become unavailable, and new methods are only slowly being made available in the United States. Some are being kept off the market because of fear that they function as aborti-facients, while the new methods being approved are raising questions of availability and appropriateness for all population groups.

One initial issue is that the amount of research being funded in new birth control devices is decreasing. Until 1980 at least nine large pharmaceutical companies were carrying on research on contraceptive development, but only one is still doing so (Hilts, 1990). Reasons for the decline in research include negative publicity from the pro-life movement, and fear of legal suits due to complications of new tech-niques. This fear is not totally ungrounded since several large product liability suits have been won against the manufacturers of birth control devices.

The decrease in private funding of contraceptive research by drug companies has not been balanced by an increase in federal funds. In fact, the amount of federal funding for research on contraception is very small when compared with other health problems. In fiscal year 1991, the federal government spent $750 million for AIDS research and only $20 million for contraceptive research ("The U.S. Contraceptive Gap," 1991). Research using fetal tissue and fertilized human eggs has been the subject of enormous controversy because of the links to abortion. Thus one success of those groups opposed to abortion has been a decline in research on birth control.

None of the major drug and device manufacturers now produces an IUD in the United States. Ortho stopped marketing the Lippes Loop in 1985, followed by Searle and Company taking the copper related IUDs off the U.S. market in 1986 (they are still distributed internationally). These were the most commonly used IUDs, and now only one, which also releases a hormone, is available from a small producer. These devices were not removed because of new findings of medical risks, but because of economics (Forrest, 1986). The financial risks of potential lawsuits for any negative outcomes were too great in the United States. Thus the lack of IUDs is related to problems in product liability insurance and potential lawsuits.

One major new contraceptive, RU 486, produced by a French drug company, is commercially available in France and China and is being tested in Great Britain and Scandinavia ("The U.S. Contraceptive Gap," 1991). This medication is popularly known as the abortion pill because it interrupts pregnancy by blocking the action of progesterone, the female hormone that prepares the uterine lining for a fertilized egg. It is not being marketed in the United States. Anti-abortion groups have threatened massive boycotts of other products of the French company in the United States and have also threatened liability lawsuits. The Food and Drug Administration (FDA) has banned import of it, even for research purposes, saying that women might then use it without adequate physician supervision (typically, in France four visits are part of the request, use of, and follow-up to the use of the drug). Most sources believe political pressure on the FDA and fear of lawsuits by the drug companies are the major reason the drug will not even be tested in the United States ("The U.S. Contraceptive Gap," 1991). In addition, injectable contraceptives, such as Depo-Provera, have long been available in other countries but not in the United States.

The first new major contraceptive medication to be approved since the pill is Norplant, a new way of delivering progestin, an antifertility hormone contained in birth control pills. It is implanted in the arm of a woman and lasts for 5 years. It has a high degree of effectiveness and is reversible by removal of the implants ("New contraceptive," 1991). It has already been approved for use in 16 other countries. Controversies about its use relate to whether state Medicaid programs will pay for the insertion of the device (costs of $350 to $600); whether they will pay for the removal if a woman on Medicaid and welfare then wishes to become pregnant; and the ordering of its insertion by a California judge in the case of a woman who had abused her children. The issue of forced sterilization has long been controversial, and this method now raises a concern over possible forced use of long-term contraceptives.

Policies Over New Reproductive Technologies

The other side of reproductive health policy from preventing births is assisting births. Current estimates are that more than 20,000 couples in the United States each year now conceive with the help of genetic material donated by a third or fourth party. These situations include the fairly noncontroversial use of donated sperm, and the use of donated ova (eggs), donated entire embryos, and surrogate mothers. The use of these alternative reproductive technologies, other than sperm donation, is not well regulated yet by state legal codes (Donovan, 1986; Ross, 1990). The *Stern v. Whitehead* case of Baby M, in which a surrogate mother wished to keep the child, has made some states begin to legislate on this issue and has raised to new complexities some aspects of contractual relationships (Field, 1988).

Some feminist researchers have pointed out that Whitehead was a "surrogate" mother only if we believe that babies, by definition, belong to the biological father, and that motherhood is simply a honorific title (Rothman, 1989). This approach is critical of the emphasis on production in the new technologies and the removal of the mother from the process. Newer legal decisions have again raised the issue of what the definition of parenthood is. In October 1990, a judge in California denied parental rights to a surrogate mother, who had carried and given birth to an implanted fetus with which she had no genetic connection, comparing her to a foster parent and raising the issue Rothman warns about, that of viewing women merely as wombs to be rented (Mydans, 1990). Another new medical advance makes it possible for a woman past menopause age to carry and give birth to an implanted embryo that is a genetic stranger to her. Thus new and thoughtful approaches to definitions of parenthood are required to advert further controversial lawsuits. Public opinion on these issues is neither settled nor uniform, however, creating a situation of possible political controversy.

Abortion Controversy

There are a number of controversies about current abortion policy. One is the fundamental debate about whether abortion should continue to be legal or be banned in the United States, except in limited circumstances. Much of this debate is a moral one, with one side arguing that abortion is the killing of a live person and that accepting abortion places us on the slippery slope that can lead to the acceptance of the killing of other defenseless groups (Rodman et al., 1987). This side tends to focus on the rights of the fetus. The other side focuses on the rights of women to determine whether and when they become mothers. Morally, this side views the rights of the currently living person, the woman, as paramount and also views the fetus as only a potential life. Thus they argue abortion is not that different from birth control, which also prevents the development of potential life. A more limited issue, but very important as regards continued availability of abortion while it remains legal, is the decline in the number of providers willing to and knowledgeable on how to perform abortions, and also issues of access to the poor. This section will review the more limited issues first, after setting the context of the debate that has occurred since the Supreme Court's 1973 *Roe v. Wade* decision, which effectively legalized abortion in the United States.

Although that decision initially resulted in greatly improved access to abortion, lower costs, and the feeling that abortion would cease to be the controversial issue that it had become in the 1960s, the fight over abortion rights has actually become more strident, and even violent at times (Joffe, 1991). Particularly with the election of Ronald Reagan as president in 1980, political and social conservatives, typified by the Moral Majority, viewed a number of changes in American society as threatening to their image of the family and society. These trends included permissive sexual attitudes, changing gender roles, family patterns such as the increase of women in the labor force, and abortion.

Initial thrusts of the anti-abortion or Right to Life movement were to raise questions of who had to consent to an abortion, particularly whether either a husband's consent or parental consent for minors should be required. In addition, another thrust was to restrict the availability of abortion to poor women who needed abortions paid for with federal funds. Because the Court did not rule on issues of waiting periods and consent, a number of states passed restrictions along these lines. Through 1986 the courts generally supported a woman's right to abortion without outside interference. This was truer for the issue of women being able to decide without the permission of a husband. In the case of minors, many lower courts have upheld statues that required parental notification, and even consent, as long as there were options for emancipated minors (minors who are largely independent of their parents) and a route for minors to demonstrate to the courts that they are mature enough to make the decision on their own (Rodman et al., 1987).

The battle over use of public funds has been a major source of controversy. Opponents of abortion were outraged that their federal tax dollars were being used to provide abortions. Their complaints have been translated into legislation and now it is prohibited to use foreign aid money in support of abortion and to pay for lawyers in public service to help clients secure abortions. The largest controversy has focused upon the Medicaid program's providing health services to the poor. In 1976, $45 million in federal funds paid for more than 250,000 abortions for poor women, 25% of all abortions in the United States that year. Initial attempts by states to restrict the use of state Medicaid funds for abortion were overturned by the courts (Linton, 1990). In 1976 Congress passed the Hyde Amendment, which bars the use of federal funds for abortion under the Medicaid program, except where the life of the mother would be endangered. The law withstood a constitutional challenge. By 1978 only 2,500 abortions were covered by federal Medicaid funds. Only 13 states now pay for abortions for low-income women. The third type of restrictions has been procedural requirements and waiting periods. Generally, waiting periods have been connected with informed consent requirements and initially were struck down by the courts during the first trimester.

One impact of the lack of federal funding and the increased controversy over performing abortions has been the increased reluctance of many physicians to perform them. At present, abortions can only be performed if physicians are willing to do them (Lamanna, 1991; Roth, 1991). The increased politicization of abortion and the picketing of abortion sites and attempts to prevent women from entering such facilities, which have even included bomb threats, have decreased the numbers of physicians willing to perform abortions. In some instances, there has even been picketing of schools attended by children of physicians who perform abortions. As a result of such strident tactics, many training programs no longer teaching physicians how to perform abortions. In addition, since most abortions today occur in a clinic or doctor's office (more than 90% in 1988, versus only half in 1973), it is harder for physicians who are mostly trained through in-hospital services to receive adequate practice in the technique.

Even in the initial period after *Roe v. Wade*, counties containing one-fourth of the U.S. population had no physicians who performed abortions (Roth, 1991). Eighty-three percent of all U.S. counties now have no hospital or clinic providing abortions (Lewin, 1992). Table 4.3 indicates the number, ratio, and rate of abortions in each state in 1988, as well as the percentage of abortions obtained by out-of-state residents, and documents the wide variations across states.

The number of rural abortion providers declined 51% from the peak level of 1977, with a 19% decline between 1985 and 1988. The number of urban providers dropped 6% from 1982 to 1988 (Wann, 1990). Hospitals in particular are eliminating abortion services. Several rural states, such as North and South Dakota, have no hospitals providing abortions. The site of abortions has shifted greatly, from 52% being performed in hospitals in 1973 to only 10% in 1988 (Lewin, 1992). Many younger physicians may not know how to perform abortions, since only 13% of obstetrics-gynecology residencies now require training in first trimester abortions, and only 7% require training in second trimester abortions, versus one-fourth of such programs in 1985, and the majority in the mid-1970s.

How does the public now view abortion? One quick summary would be that since 1960 there has been agreement about the appropriateness of legal abortions for medical reasons, such as danger to the mother and fetal deformity, except on the part of the most extreme segment of the population. There is less consistency of public support for nonmedical reasons, such as the woman is not married or does not want any more children at this time or does not want this baby at this particular time (Rodman et al., 1987). Looking across time from the 1960s on, favorable attitudes toward abortion changed little across the 1960s, became more favorable in the early 1770s, then stabilized again, and began to decline in the 1980s.

Why did favorable attitudes decline in the 1980s? The president was outspoken in his opposition, as was the Pope and a prominent Roman Catholic nun, Mother Theresa, who won the Nobel Peace Prize in 1979. In addition, the overall political climate in the United States has become more conservative. Nevertheless, public opinion does not support the Right to Life movement's position of a complete ban on abortion, since in 1985 about 90% of the public supported abortion if a woman's health was endangered, and about 80% in cases of rape or serious defect in the baby. Even for reasons such as a low income and not being able to afford the baby, or an unmarried woman not wanting to marry the father, 40% of the public support abortion (Rodman et al.). A 1990 public opinion poll reveals the deep inconsistencies and conflict about this issue among Americans. Seventy-three percent of those polled were in favor of abortion rights, but 77% also regarded abortion as a kind of killing, and 28% solely as the taking of a human life (Rosenblatt, 1992). These differences can occur in polls because most Americans support abortion as a principle in some circumstances, but are against abortion as their own personal choice in many situations.

One major change in the past few years has been the 1989 *Webster v. Reproductive Health Services* decision. While the immediate impact of this decision on most abortions performed in the United States is minimal, the overall impact of the decision is major (Linton, 1990). The decision affirmed the constitutionality of restrictions on the use of public facilities or public employees in the performance of abortions not necessary to save the life of the mother, thus denying the claim of a constitutional right of access to public facilities for abortion. It also upheld a section of the law requiring a mandated determination of viability prior to the performance of an abortion after 20 weeks of gestation. The Court refused to pass judgment on the constitutionality of the preamble language of the original law, that life begins at conception and that unborn children had protectable legal interests under Missouri law (Linton, 1990). One question with this challenge was whether the Court would begin to dismantle the trimester framework of *Roe*.

In the *Webster* decision, four justices were willing to reject this framework but not the fifth required for a majority. One consistent change across the decade of the '80s has been that the Court majority supporting abortion has become smaller, from the 7 to 2 decision of *Roe v. Wade* to the 5 to 4 decision of *Webster*, reflecting the voting patterns of the Reagan and Bush appointees (Fried, 1990). Many experts believe that *Roe v. Wade* will be overturned in the next few years, creating a situation in which access to abortion will again be directed by state laws.

What is the future of access to abortion in the United States? How does it relate to overall health policy? Clearly, there is a lack of consensus on this issue. Also clearly, as in the past when abortions were illegal but perhaps even more so today, given greater knowledge and faster means of transportation, the declaring of the trimester framework of *Roe v. Wade* invalid and the passage by some states of extremely restrictive abortion laws would not mean that no abortions are available in the United States. Some states would pass laws making abortion legal. Some women would return to illegal abortions, probably leading to more deaths from poorly performed abortions. Given the realities of economics, more of these women would be poor and poorly educated, thus increasing social inequity. Some experts fear that the overturn of *Roe v. Wade* would lead to mayhem and increased political conflict (Fried, 1990; Rosenblatt, 1992). Rosenblatt argues that public opinion data indicate that most Americans want abortion legal, but want to discourage its practice. Thus Congress should pass a law protecting the right to abortion, as did the *Roe v. Wade* decision, but increase funding for contraceptives and birth control education that would decrease its practice. Rosenblatt believes political leadership is called for, rather than turning the issue over to the courts and allowing elected leaders to avoid taking a stand on the issue. The future of abortion as one option for reproductive choices in American remains a major controversy.

5

Aging and Long-Term Care

The aging of the U.S. population is one of the most important social trends of the past half-century and also of the next 50 years. Related to the aging of the population are increased needs for health care services, including regular physician care, hospital-based care, and perhaps particularly important, long-term care. Long-term care includes care for chronic and other conditions in which the goal of most treatment is control and maintenance, not cure. The types of services included under long-term care are nursing home services; medically oriented home health services, such as visiting nursing care and physical therapy; and homemaker-type home care services, such as meal preparation and light housekeeping. In addition, special services, such as congregate living facilities with congregate meals and special retirement communities with medical assistance available, represent other possible types of long-term care.

In some ways, policy in this area presents less controversy than in some other areas of health care. This may be because there is wide agreement on certain basic premises about aging in American society. These include the belief that elderly Americans have a right to health care (which has partially been enacted into law through the federal Medicare program) and to not be impoverished by the costs of health care as they become older. Another widely shared belief is that the elderly have a right to care beyond traditional inpatient and doctor care currently provided through Medicare. Medicare will cover a number of medically related home care services now, such as home nursing visits, physical therapists, and health aides. In addition, the federally funded Area Agencies on Aging (AAA) currently provide another group of services. Examples of some of the services funded through that mechanism include transportation services for the elderly, Meals on Wheels, senior centers, various types of adult day care, respite services, and homemaker chore services (Coward & Cutler, 1989). Other generally shared values in the society, although less formalized by any particular program, focus on the importance to the elderly of having friends and relatives nearby if possible, of being able to stay in one's own home or a home of one's choosing as one ages, and of keeping as healthy and active as possible.

There are also some major areas of controversy or less generally shared values, but many of these relate more to how to provide and finance care than the goal of providing care. In some cases, there is fairly good consensus on certain goals, but not on the complete approach to achieve the goals. For example, most people agree on the importance of quality as one factor in long-term care, but not necessarily on how these services should be delivered or paid for. Should it be an expense that people save for or buy long-term care insurance for, or should it be provided by the government much as hospital and physician care now are by Medicare? Other concerns on which there is more controversy relate to how states and the federal government should balance their financial obligations to the elderly versus other population groups, issues of death and dying and the rights of the elderly to make personal choices in this regard, and the linkages between gender and aging and aging services. In this area, there are controversies, especially about the obligations of female relatives and appropriate expectations for care that those women might provide to a generation older than themselves. Linked to this is the question of the obligations of families, in which the controversy relates less to whether families should feel a sense of obligation than to what ought to happen to the elderly whose families are not an important presence, either due to no family near or no family existing, the lack of concern of that family, or the lack of means of those families to provide care and help with care despite concern.

Trends in the Aging of the U.S. Population

One reason why issues of aging and long-term care are increasingly important for health care policy in general are changes in the proportion of the population that is elderly, often defined as 65 and over. In addition, the composition of the elderly is itself changing over time, both in the age distribution and gender. At the turn of the century, the elderly defined as people over 65 were only a small part of the U.S. population, about 4% (Public Health Service, 1990). By 1988 that proportion had increased to 12.4%. Estimates are that more than 20% of the U.S. population will be over 65 years of age by the year 2020. Moreover, the most rapidly increasing segment of the U.S. population is people 85 and older, predominantly women.

Why are there so many more elderly now than before? At the turn of the century, the United States was still an immigrant nation, and immigrants historically are younger people, not the elderly. Also, few people lived as long in the past as is typical now, with the average life expectancy at birth in 1900 around 50, increasing to 68 by 1950, and to 75 by 1987 (Estes & Phillip, 1986; Public Health Service, 1990). Thus people are living longer, partially due to control of infectious diseases earlier in life and pneumonia in middle life, and for the past 30 years, due to advances in medical care such that people who formerly died with a first stroke or heart attack now may live with the chronic health problem another 20 or 30 years.

Who the elderly are is also changing. Two important changing factors are gender and ethnicity. In 1900 life expectancy at birth was about equal for men and women, 48 years for men and 51 for women. Now there is a substantial gender gap in life expectancy, with the figures being 78 for women and 71 for men (Ory & Warners, 1990). This means that aging is increasingly an issue for women. Already, there are three older women for every two older men. At ages 75 to 79, there are more than 10 women for every 7 men, and over age 80, there are 10 women for every 5 men (U.S. Bureau of the Census, 1986a). Given marital patterns of younger women marrying older men and the longer life expectancy for women, most older men are married and live in a family setting, whereas most older women are widowed. For those 75 and over, more than half the women are living alone, while less than one-fifth of the men are (U.S. Senate Special Committee on Aging, 1988). Moreover, there is some evidence that women live longer with disabilities than do men. In one study, at every level of impairment, females lived longer than men so that the prevalence of numbers of women with disabilities continues to increase across the age spectrum (Manton, 1990). Thus issues of special housing, home health services, and even nursing home services are disproportionately a problem for women.

Currently, the elderly are disproportionately white, compared to the total population. Partially this is due to the historical association of migration with younger populations. It is also related to generally shorter life expectancies among minority groups. Fourteen percent of the white population is 65 and over, versus 8% of the black population, 6% of Asian/Pacific Islanders, and 5% each of Hispanics and Native Americans (Rivas & Torres-Gil, 1991). There may be special policy issues as these populations begin to age and life expectancies improve in minority groups. One major question is whether patterns of care will be different for these groups. There is currently evidence that minority groups use fewer nursing home services and formal aging-related services than do whites. Are these differences in preferences for care due to lack of money to pay for formal care services, or due to lack of knowledge of the available services? These are research issues to be examined in the near future, so that appropriate policy can then be implemented.

Critically important issues for aging and long-term care policy generally are the health status of the elderly and how much health care they use. While people 65 and older have 16.4 years of life remaining on average, they have only about 12 years of healthy life remaining (Public Health Service, 1990). The heavy utilizers of long-term care services in particular, but also other health care services, are those with chronic illnesses and functional disabilities. Both of these are interrelated and increase with age. Of people under 19, only 2.3% are limited in performing basic activities due to chronic illness. Of people under 45, as shown in Table 5.1, 7.2% have some type of activity limitation. By 55 to 64, 22% are limited in activity to some degree. For people 65 and over, almost 40% have some type of activity limitation, and 24% have a limitation in a major activity. For those 74 and older, figures are even higher, with 36% limited in major activities due to chronic illness (Manton & Soldo, 1985). The presence of major activity limitations does not vary that much by sex and race, again shown in Table 5.1, but is related to income, so that the presence of limitations in major activities almost triples for those in the lowest income category of under $20,000, versus the highest of $35,000 and over. At this time, medicine has become fairly proficient at keeping people alive, but not necessarily at keeping people alive in a healthy state. As positive health behaviors, such as exercise, improve, these may help to keep people active and healthy longer as they age, although there is a limit to the success of such approaches at limiting disability. This is particularly true for

Table 5.1 Persons With Activity Limitation, by Selected Chronic Conditions: 1985.

(Covers civilian noninstitutional population. Conditions classified according to 9th revision of International Classification of Diseases. Based on National Health Interview Survey.)

Condition	Total[1]	Age Under 45 years	45-64 years	65 years and over	Sex Male	Female	Race White	Black	Family Income Under $20,000	$20,000-$34,999	$35,000 and over
Persons with limitations (mll)	32.7	11.6	10.4	10.7	15.3	17.4	28.0	4.1	16.6	7.1	4.7
Percent limited by:											
Heart conditions	17.4	4.7	21.5	27.1	18.2	16.7	17.5	16.9	21.5	14.4	14.8
Arthritis and rheumatism	18.9	5.4	22.8	29.7	12.4	24.6	18.9	20.3	25.0	14.3	13.5
Hypertension[2]	10.5	2.9	15.2	14.2	7.9	12.8	9.0	21.3	15.1	7.0	5.3
Impairment of back/spine	9.2	12.5	10.4	4.4	8.9	9.4	9.4	7.0	9.1	11.0	10.6
Impairment of lower extremities and hips	8.9	10.7	8.2	7.8	9.4	8.5	9.0	8.1	10.1	8.5	9.6
Percent of all persons with:											
No activity limitation	86.0	92.8	76.6	60.4	86.4	85.6	85.9	85.5	79.7	89.2	91.9
Activity limitation	14.0	7.2	23.4	39.6	13.6	14.4	14.1	14.5	20.3	10.8	8.1
In major activity	9.5	4.9	17.5	24.1	9.7	9.4	9.4	11.1	14.2	7.3	5.1

[1] Includes persons with unknown family income and other races, not shown separately.
[2] Covers all cases of hypertension, regardless of other conditions.
SOURCE: National Center for Health Statistics, *Vital and Health Statistics*, Series 10, and unpublished data taken from *Statistical Abstract of the U.S.*, 1991, p. 121.

sensory problems linked with aging, for which we currently have few preventive approaches. Sensory problems such as hearing and vision loss become more common in the population 65 and over and are an increasingly important source of disability, so that by age 85 most elderly have some sensory limitations.

One critical and controversial question is the argument over "compression of morbidity" within the later years of life (Fries, Green, & Levine, 1989). Modern medicine allows many individuals to be kept alive through long years of disability and illness, but the majority retain vigor and ability to function into old age. Some researchers argue that the upper boundary of life expectancy has already been reached and that the new frontier of medicine is seeing whether we can postpone the onset of disability to shortly before death (Fries et al., 1989). The implications for the need for health care services are huge, depending upon whether it becomes possible for most elderly to be healthy until close to the point at which they die, or whether current patterns of increased disability with age continue or even increase as ability to keep people alive with very serious chronic illnesses increases.

Medicare and Its Limitations

One of the most misunderstood aspects of the Medicare program is how extensive and complete its coverage is for all health care costs. Whether Medicare coverage should be more extensive is one of the major health policy issues for the next decade. Medicare is the broadest social health insurance program the federal government operates, covering more that 95% of those 65 and over, as well as disabled persons under 65 who meet certain criteria and those with end-stage renal disease. The rules of what care is actually covered are quite complex, but generally physician services, inpatient care, and limited post-hospitalization care in a nursing home or through home health services are covered. Medicare does not cover most long-term care services, out-of-institution drugs, dental care, eyeglasses, hearing aids, or other medical devices.

In addition, Medicare has required cost-sharing since its inception. The patient must pay an inpatient hospital deductible each year that approximates the cost of one day of hospital care (around $600 in 1990 and generally increasing each year) and some of the co-insurance for long stays and portions of the physician bill for an inpatient stay. For outpatient care, Medicare usually covers only part of the bill and begins to pay only after a basic deductible (minimum expense) has been paid by the elderly each year. Generally, a 20% co-payment is required for the physician bill. In addition, Medicare pays nothing toward medications, a very important health cost for the elderly. The outpatient coverage (often called Part B, in contrast to the inpatient coverage feature, Part A) requires a monthly premium, which has also been increasing each year, is generally deducted from Social Security payments, and was close to $30 in 1990. Under current law, physicians may bill Medicare patients up to 20% more than the charges approved by Medicare, with the patient responsible for paying the difference.

There are supplemental health insurance policies, often known as Medigap policies, and a high proportion of middle-class and above elderly purchase these policies. In general, these policies help to pay for the basic inpatient deductible and the 20% co-insurance on physician bills, but not the physician services deductible. Better ones provide partial coverage of prescription drugs. What they do not cover (often to the surprise of some elderly) is extended stays in long-term care facilities. Thus, on average, the out-of-pocket expenses of the elderly are not that different now from what they were before Medicare was passed in 1965. This often-quoted fact does not take account of inflation, however, so the proportion of health care expenses paid directly by the elderly has decreased greatly. Nevertheless, for many people living on fixed incomes, constant increases in deductibles and co-payments make them fearful of being unable to pay their medical bills, even with Medicare. When they discover that nursing home and home health coverage are quite limited, many elderly again fear that a serious chronic illness requiring a nursing home stay would bankrupt them. While Medicare coverage means that the elderly have the highest proportion of the population of any age group with some health insurance coverage, the percentage of their income the elderly spend on health care is double to triple what other age groups spend—between 9% and 15%, depending on the study (McCall, Rice, Boismier, & West, 1991; Pollack, 1988). Many health policy experts believe that one factor that led to the passage and then repeal of the Medicare Catastrophic Act of 1988 was the awareness by the elderly that the act did not cover long-term care, but would increase the costs of the Medicare program to the typical middle-class elderly (McCall, Knickman, & Bauer, 1991).

The Relationship Between
High Health Care Costs and Aging

One aspect of the relationship between high health care costs and aging, the link with chronic health conditions and disabilities, has already been discussed. A second link is the cost of medical care during a person's last year of life. About two-thirds of the people who die each year are Medicare recipients. The Medicare recipients who die are generally only about 5% of enrollees, but account for 28% of Medicare expenditures (Lubitz & Prihoda, 1983). Another way to understand these figures is that Medicare spends six times as much in an average year on enrollees in their last year of life as on enrollees who do not die during the year. To some extent, these expenses are even more concentrated, in that almost half the costs for people who die in the year occur in the last 60 days of life (Lubitz & Prihoda, 1983). Thus one important connection between high health care costs and the elderly is that the elderly die at a higher rate than other age groups. While this sounds simplistic and obvious, it helps to point out that the costs of care for many elderly are not that different from other age groups. The high average is due to the large number of people with very high costs who die in a given year.

The other explanation for high costs is the presence of chronic health problems that require frequent health care, including long-term care services. Again, one finding is that only a small proportion of people over 65 use specialized services. Only 5% of people over 65 are residents of a nursing home on any given day (Hing, 1987), the largest single group of whom are 85 and over. Seventy-five percent of nursing home residents are female, and 93% are white (Hing, Sekscenski, & Stahan, 1989). Most nursing home residents are elderly, more than 90%, with almost half over age 85 (Pepper Commission, 1990). Even for people over 85, only 20% are in a nursing home at any one point in time. The chances of ever being in a nursing home are much higher, with estimates that 25% to 40% of all older persons will enter a nursing home at least once (Evashwick, 1988). The probabilities are higher for women than men. More than half of the women will probably spend time in a nursing home, versus one-third of the men (Pepper Commission, 1990). Thus the very high costs of nursing home care are concentrated on a small subgroup of people.

One major controversy is how to pay for this care. Medicare pays for only 2% to 3% of nursing home care. Currently, slightly less than half is paid for by individuals and the same amount by Medicaid, the program for the poor which becomes the payor once people exhaust all their other resources. Many elderly who were not poor throughout their adult lives nevertheless become eligible for Medicaid for nursing home care through a procedure known as "spending down." Once a person spends all resources, leaving a small amount for a spouse if still alive, he or she can become Medicaid eligible. Two types of controversies relate to this procedure. For many elderly, who are proud of having always been self-sufficient, to become eligible for a "welfare" program is disturbing and a blow to the ego. Yet some elderly with resources transfer those assets to others, creating room for potential fraud and abuse of the spend-down procedure. But it is the fear of being impoverished by these costs that haunts most elderly, making coverage for such care not only a major political goal of many elderly but also a major controversy in the health care system.

The estimates of one recent study, about the future costs of nursing home care for Americans who will turn 65 in 1990, reinforce these concerns and fears. This study estimated that nursing home care for these people will cost $60 billion (Kemper, Spillman, & Murtaugh, 1991). Because nursing home costs keep increasing, each person in the country would have to invest $27,600 at a rate of more than 5% of the nursing home inflation rate (such high-paying investments are currently not available) and then pool all those resources to cover the estimated costs of nursing home care for those elderly who end up needing it. At the lower rates of interest currently available, much larger sums would need to be invested. The authors estimate that recently proposed alternative strategies to pay for nursing home care through private insurance or public entitlement would cover no more than 59% of the costs under the best of assumptions, leaving the remainder, as it is under current policy, to be covered by the elderly themselves, their families, or an existing public program such as Medicaid (Kemper et al., 1991). Thus how to pay for nursing home coverage remains a difficult and controversial issue.

All types of community-based services have become a major growth area in long-term care. Again, a relatively small proportion of the elderly (about 22%) use community services in a given year (Stone, 1986). The most frequently used service is the community senior center, used by 15% of the elderly. According to a large national survey conducted in 1984, only 1% of the elderly living in the community used in-home services. Most experts believe the figure is up some now, due to reimbursement changes for hospital care that encourage earlier discharge from the hospital, thus requiring more use of in-home services. Use of such services increases with age and among those living alone (Stone, 1986).

The Array of Elderly Services:
Where Should They Be Provided?

In addition to Medicare, another federal act passed in 1965, the Older Americans Act (OAA), provides an underpinning for some other elderly related services. This program is administered by the Administration on Aging in the Department of Health and Human Services and has been instrumental in developing a nationwide infrastructure of helping older persons, including 57 State Units on Aging and 670 Area Agencies on Aging (Binstock, 1991). All persons 60 and older are eligible for these services. The types of services included under this act include nutrition services, senior centers, and a broad range of supportive and outreach services. While the organizations created under this act are very important in creating a network of aging-related services, the dollar amounts allocated have not kept up with the inflation rate, and using inflation-adjusted appropriations figures, OAA appropriations reached a peak in 1981 and have declined substantially in constant dollars since then (Binstock, 1991). Thus only 0.1% of the total cost of long-term care services are met by this act (Howard, 1991).

Where should long-term care services be provided? One trend of the 1980s was a major growth in home care services. This trend reflects pressures on hospitals to control patient flow under new reimbursement systems, an increased demand from the elderly population, and the desire by both consumers and payors to minimize health care costs by substituting less-expensive home-based services for nursing home care (Evashwick, 1988). There are currently four persons using community based services for every person in a nursing home (Ory & Duncker, 1992). Yet the limited evidence available supports the assumption that most older people and their families prefer in-home or community-based assistance. One survey of people on a waiting list at a continuing-care retirement community found that reasons for joining were to assure access to services, to maintain independence, and to avoid being a burden to one's family (Tell, Cohen, Larson, & Batten, 1987). A

Canadian study found that 57% of the elderly preferred to live alone or with their spouse, and if they had to live with someone else, relatives were the first choice (Beland, 1987).

How to pay on an extended basis for long-term care services is a major issue. While Medicare, Medicaid, and the OAA all cover some aspects of home care, not all services are covered. A related important factor is that currently most of the care given in the home is informal care by friends and relatives. Less than 10% of informal caregivers report the use of paid help (Noelker & Bass, 1989). While this may be good from a cost perspective, among the growing problems are caregiver burnout and lack of coordination between types of care. Also, most of the actual care provision to elderly is performed by female relatives. As the labor force participation rates of women increase, there will be fewer women available to provide these unpaid services to the elderly. One major controversy in future policy deliberations is the extent to which there needs to be a way to better coordinate different types of care, and possibly even reimburse relatives or friends for care provision, especially if it means decreasing labor force activity.

If home-based services are not available, nursing homes will have to remain as a fallback location of care for those without adequate community support or with too low a level of functioning. Paying for nursing home care is a major policy concern. The possibility of individuals saving enough for their own care is not practical for most people (Kemper et al., 1991). Private long-term care insurance has not been that successful, and it often provides specific dollar benefits that, even with some inflation adjustment, have not been keeping up with the rate of inflation in nursing home cost. Thus most such policies will cover only a limited portion of the expense. Paying for nursing home care remains a controversial issue.

The other controversial issues in nursing home care are quality of care and the types of providers. More than 80% of all nursing home care is now provided in for-profit facilities. Nursing homes in most parts of the country average 95% occupancy rates and are quite profitable (Kronenfeld & Whicker, 1990). There is some evidence that nonprofit facilities (especially church-related ones) have higher quality of care. Patients paid for by public funds are mostly in for-profit facilities, however. Thus concern about cost containment may conflict with quality concerns, creating a complex set of policy considerations.

The Right to Die Controversy

One very controversial area in aging today concerns what freedom patients should have in determining how long they are kept alive and when they should die. For the past 20 years, the idea that patients should indicate whether they wish to be maintained on life support has been gaining acceptance through the use of "Living Wills." In fact, health care facilities are now required to obtain information about such wishes from patients. A term often used is *passive euthanasia*, a situation in which medical care providers, in accordance with the previously stated wishes of a patient, do not keep a person alive through machines and technology if the person's body is not capable of sustaining life without assistance.

Far more controversial is the issue of whether patients should be allowed to engage in "active euthanasia" and whether physicians and health care providers should participate in such actions. The rate of suicide among the elderly is increasing, with a 21% jump from 1980 to 1986 (Ingram, 1992). A major best-seller published in 1992 is a book explaining methods for suicide among the elderly, written by one of the founders of the Hemlock Society, a group supportive of active euthanasia (Case, 1991). In 1991 there was an initiative on the ballot in the state of Washington to allow doctor-assisted suicides (Case, 1991). Although the measure failed, that situation and the participation of a Michigan physician, Jack Kevorkian, in several different assisted deaths or suicides have made this one of the most controversial issues in aging care currently. In Holland, terminally ill patients can receive a lethal injection from their doctors, and about 5,000 to 10,000 such procedures are performed each year (Rosenbaum, 1991). Kevorkian has already been on trial for assisted suicide once in his home state (Rosenbaum, 1991). One major concern is that the most difficult or costly patients will be pushed toward suicide. Others contend that regulations to allow doctor-assisted suicides would be compassionate and consistent with medical ethics, if appropriately regulated (Ingram, 1992). This issue raises some of the most basic questions of moral and religious beliefs regarding the sanctity of life, as well as the potential for undue pressure on patients.

Generational Equity Issues

A last growing controversy in aging is the notion of intergenerational equity and how much in tax dollars should be spent on care for the elderly. In 1965, when Medicare and the OAA were passed, there was a compassionate attitude toward the elderly and the dying as part of an era of expanded social programs (Binstock, 1991). Currently, a new set of images depict older persons as prosperous, active, hedonistic and selfish. One reads in the popular media such terms as *greedy geezers*, terms reinforced by bumper stickers seen in retirement areas that proclaim, "We are spending our children's inheritance." Clearly, this new image reflects stereotyping. Partially, however, the real situation of the elderly has changed. In 1965 one-third of those 65 and older were living in poverty. Today only 12% do (McConnell & Beitler, 1991). The largest single group by age now living in poverty is children.

Linked to changing trends of poverty are growing trends of public expenditures on the elderly. Expenditures for persons 65 and older (12.6% of the population in 1989), accounted for more than 28% of the annual federal budget (Binstock, 1991). People 65 and older account for one-third of the nation's annual health care expenditures. In addition, the elderly have become at times an effective voting bloc, and groups such as the AARP, the American Association for Retired Persons, have become active in lobbying for elderly related benefits in Congress. This issue has been raised as a question of intergenerational equity. How much of the resources of the nation should be invested in one particular age group? This issue remains controversial, with no easy answers, and may become more critical beginning in the next century as the large population bulge of baby boomers begins to reach retirement age.

6

Providers of Care
Health Professions
and Health Facilities

M ost of the previous chapters have dealt with specific age groups and their health care problems, or with specific disease related health care issues. This chapter will deal with policies and controversies about providers of health care. Generally, providers can be divided into two types: people who actually provide care, such as physicians and nurses, and places that provide care, such as hospitals and outpatient care settings. This chapter will initially discuss policies and controversies related to the health professions and health personnel. The rest of the chapter will predominantly concentrate on policy issues and controversies relating to places in which care is provided.

Health Professions and Health Personnel

Different Types of Health Personnel

The number of different types of health care professionals and the growth in numbers of people employed in the health care system have increased dramatically in the twentieth century. In 1910 only 1.3% of all employed people were in the health care sector. By 1950 this had almost doubled, to 2.5%, and then doubled again in the next 30 years, up to 5.2% by 1980 (Moscovice, 1988). Currently, the health care industry is the largest single employer of all the industries monitored by the Department of Labor, outpacing overall employment in the economy and total population growth. Thus health personnel policy is important both for its role in adequate delivery of health care and for its role in the overall economy as a major employer.

Not only have the numbers of people employed in health care increased, but the types of people have changed and the numbers of different categories of health care workers have increased. Physicians, registered nurses, pharmacists, and dentists were major categories of health care providers in 1910. Over the years, new groups have been added, some, such as optometrists, podiatrists, and physical therapists, with fairly high levels of specialized training. In addition, many new categories have been created, especially in the past 30 years, such as physicians' assistants, dental hygienists, laboratory technicians, practical nurses, nursing aides, home health aides, medical records personnel, respiratory therapists, and many other categories of allied health and support service personnel. There are now more than 700 different job categories in the health industry.

Actually, it is the newer categories of health care providers that have increased the most in numbers. The traditional health care occupations of physicians, dentists, pharmacists, and optometrists have experienced dramatic declines in their relative proportion of all health care personnel, although the absolute numbers have increased in the past 30 years. More than two-thirds of all personnel now employed in health care are in nontraditional allied health or support service positions (Moscovice, 1988). One reason for this is the growth in technological innovation in the health care system in the past 30 years. As new types of machinery become available, often new allied health positions are created to specialize in the new area of medicine and new technology. This has been combined with both ever-increasing trends of specialization within the profession of medicine itself and an emergence of the hospital as the primary setting for the implementation of new technology. One traditional health care occupation, registered nursing, has continued to grow in large numbers. Registered nurses currently represent the largest single group of health care personnel. Given their group's size and importance, there are specific controversies about how to have enough nurses and what types of nurses will be needed in the health care system of the future.

Stratification Within Health Care Professions

Many analysts of the health labor force agree on the dominant role of physicians traditionally (Aries & Kennedy, 1990; Freidson, 1970, 1987; Starr, 1982). However, the medical profession and occupations related to it have undergone enormous changes in the past 20 to 30 years. Many believe the role of the physician is changing and dominance over other health occupations decreasing over time. More than two-thirds of all personnel now in health care are in allied health and support positions. Why is this change occurring? One factor many analysts would agree on as influencing the health labor force is changes in medical technology, which have partially been illustrated above in the figures on changes in types of health personnel (Aries & Kennedy, 1990; Banta, Behny, & Wilems, 1981; Starr, 1982). One unique aspect of the growth of technology in health care and its interaction with personnel needs is that new technology in health care often implies a new category of technical assistant to run the machine. This is unlike the trend in many production-oriented industries in which capital investment decreases labor intensity. In the health care industry, the greater the reliance on new equipment, the greater the need for additional support staff.

What are other factors changing the role of dominance of physicians? The financing of health care has been viewed by some as an important factor (Aries & Kennedy, 1990), as has the feeling that health care costs are increasing too rapidly. While the cost of physician care is only one element of rising costs, it is often a visible element. This ties in with a changed attitude by consumers and others toward health care, and more questioning of physicians, both on medical issues and cost issues, as another important factor (Freidson, 1987).

Physicians traditionally have played the dominant role in the health care occupations, setting the terms and condition of work for all the other groups. They have been the group that earned the most, hired directly or indirectly many of the other workers, and was involved in writing licensure and certification requirements and exams for many of the growing technical health occupations. Freidson (1970) has characterized physicians as being "technically autonomous," that is, being able to set their own conditions of work. Critically for policy issues with other health care occupations, physicians have also had the right to limit and evaluate the performance of most other health care workers. While the profession of medicine is undergoing challenges to its position now, which may be part of an emerging policy issue about an adequate supply of physicians, there is little question that physicians rank at the top of a hierarchy of health care occupations. Other types of workers mostly do work that helps physicians function, do not directly engage in the critical tasks of diagnosis of the problem and prescription of care, and earn far less with more limited opportunities for either advancement in earnings or diversity of job.

The growth of the consumer movement has resulted in a challenge to physicians' autonomy (Haug, 1976). Consumer trust in the advice of all types of professionals is declining, partially because the modern consumer is better educated and more likely to comprehend medical subjects, thus decreasing the knowledge gaps between consumers and health care providers.

The passage of the Medicare and Medicaid legislation in 1965 committed vast amounts of federal funds into the health care system, but also ultimately made the costs of health care more visible. At the same time as improved access was increasing total dollars in the health care system, and improved technology was raising total costs, labor costs within the health care sector became an issue. At one time, the major providers in health care were physicians, who operated as small private businessmen, and nurses, who were poorly paid, both because of the origins of the field as a charitable enterprise and because nursing was a female-dominated field, and female fields have traditionally paid more poorly within the American economy (Reverby, 1990). Nursing salaries increased in the 1960s and 1970s, as did the salaries of other less-trained hospital workers. Important factors were growth of the minimum wage and unionization movements. Because 60% of hospital costs are attributed to labor inputs, labor costs are the most likely source of savings (Aries & Kennedy, 1990). One of the current major controversies within health occupations is how to deal with tensions between various health occupations, related both to level of pay and job responsibilities.

Current Major Policy Issues

Medicine, Supply of Personnel, and Changing Roles

Having an appropriate number of physicians in practice has long been a major policy goal. Several difficulties occur in achieving this objective.

The first is determining what is the appropriate number of physicians. The second is determining what trends in supply really are, how rapidly they are changing or may change, and how these link to changing roles of physicians within the health care delivery system. The number of physicians in the United States has increased rapidly in the past two decades, with more than a 60% increase in the number of physicians in practice. Two different trends account for the increased numbers: an increase in the number of graduates from medical schools since 1965 and substantial emigration of foreign physicians to the United States. Before 1970 the general belief was that the United States had too few physicians. Historically, students graduating from U.S. medical schools had filled only two-thirds to three-quarters of all the residencies available in U.S. hospitals. Thus in the 1960s and 1970s, there were large new federal outlays for training of medical school students and construction of new medical schools to increase the supply. These polices starting to work, and numbers increased, as illustrated in Table 6.1, which shows the changes in the supply of physicians, nurses, and dentists from 1970 to 1988.

Beginning in 1980 the Graduate Medical Education National Advisory Committee (GMENAC) warned of a surplus of 70,000 physicians by 1990 (GMENAC, 1980). This conclusion was controversial at the time, with many experts arguing that it underestimated the changing patterns of medical school enrollment and preferences as to hours of work. Also, critiques included a lack of attention to short supply in certain fields, especially primary care fields such as family practice, and certain parts of the country, particularly rural areas (Barnett & Midling, 1989). The number of female medical students was increasing, and evidence was growing that both female and male young physicians desired to work fewer hours than the 60- to 80-hour work weeks typical of many older physicians. Depending upon the assumptions of how many hours the typical physician of the future will work, the estimates of physician supply vary greatly.

In general, these estimates of oversupply did not turn out to be true for 1990, and recent estimates are that at most only half as large a surplus will be available in the year 2000 as the GMENAC estimates (Weiner, 1989). Several controversies relate to such estimates from a public policy perspective. One approach argues that it is better to have too many rather than too few physicians, so that access is better and physicians are better distributed. Another more economically based argument is that excess physicians drain resources initially (based on

Table 6.1 Physicians, Dentists, and Nurses: 1970 to 1988 (Physicians, dentists, and nurses as of end of year, except as noted. Data for physicians include Puerto Rico and outlying areas)

Item	UNIT	1970	1975	1980	1982	1983	1984	1985	1986	1987	1988
Physicians number[1]	1,000	348	409	487	523	542	(NA)	577	595	612	(NA)
Rate per 10,000 population[2]	Rate	168	187	211	222	228	(NA)	237	246	252	(NA)
Doctors of medicine[3]	1,000	334	394	468	502	520	(NA)	553	569	586	(NA)
Active non-federal[4]	1,000	281	312	397	430	447	(NA)	476	484	500	(NA)
Rate per 10,000 population[4][5]	Rate	137	143	172	184	190	(NA)	201	202	205	(NA)
Active foreign medical school graduates[4][5]	1,000	54	(NA)	82	96	100	(NA)	105	107	111	(NA)
Doctors of osteopathy	1,000	14	15	19	21	22	23	24	25	27	28
Medical and osteopathic schools[7]	Number	107	123	140	142	142	142	142	142	142	142
Students[7]	1,000	39.7	57.2	70.1	72.6	73.5	73.6	73.2	72.8	72.3	71.9
Graduates[7]	1,000	8.8	13.4	16.2	17.0	17.1	17.6	17.8	17.7	17.4	17.5
Newly licensed physicians total[6][8]	1,000	11.0	16.9	18.2	17.6	20.6	18.3	18.3	19.6	(NA)	(NA)
Percent of total active MDs[9]	Percent	3.5	4.6	4.2	4.1	4.3	(NA)	3.6	3.8	(NA)	(NA)
Graduates of — U.S. and Canadian medical schools	1,000	8.0	10.9	14.9	13.4	15.8	14.2	15.3	16.7	(NA)	(NA)
Foreign medical schools	1,000	3.0	6.0	3.3	4.2	4.8	4.1	3.0	2.9	(NA)	(NA)
Percent of total newly licensed	Percent	27.3	35.4	18.2	23.8	23.1	22.3	16.7	15.0	(NA)	(NA)

Dentist, number	1,000	116	127	141	147	150	153	156	158	161	163
Active (exc. in federal service)	1,000	96	107	121	127	130	133	136	138	140	142
Rate per 10,000 population[5]	Rate	47	50	54	55	56	57	57	57	58	58
Dental schools[10]	Number	53	59	60	60	60	60	60	59	58	58
Students[10]	1,000	16.0	20.1	22.5	22.2	21.4	20.6	19.6	18.7	17.9	17.1
Graduates[1]	1,000	3.7	5.0	5.3	5.4	5.8	5.3	5.4	5.0	4.7	4.6
Nurses, number (active registered)	1,000	750	961	1,273	1,380	1,439	1,486	1,544	1,589	1,627	1,648
Rate per 100,000 population[2]	Rate	368	446	560	595	615	629	647	659	668	670
Nursing programs[11]	Number	1,340	1,362	1,385	1,432	1,466	1,477	1,473	1,469	1,465	1,442
Students[11]	1,000	163	248	231	242	251	237	218	194	183	185
Graduates[11]	1,000	46	77	76	74	77	80	82	77	71	65

NA Not available. [1] Includes not classified, inactive, and federal physicians. [2] Based on Bureau of the Census resident population estimates as of July 1. [3] Excludes non-federal physicians with temporary foreign addresses; see headnote, table 159.1987 data as of January 1, 1988. [4] Excludes nonclassified physicians. [5] Based on Bureau of the Census Civilian Population estimates as of July 1. [6] Foreign medical graduates excludes graduates of Canadian schools. [7] Based on cata from annual surveys conducted by the Association of American Medical Colleges and the American Association of Colleges of Medicine. [8] Source: American Medical Association, Chicago, IL U.S. *Medical Licensure Statistics*, 1984 and *License Requirement*, 1985, and *Physician Characteristics and Distribution in the U.S.*, Annual (Copyright). [9] Excludes M.D.s with unknown addresses. Includes those not classified. [10] Based on data from the American Dental Association, Council on Dental Education *Annual Report on Dental Education*. [11] Number of programs and students are as of October 15 and number of graduates are for academic year ending in year shown: from National League of Nursing, *NLN Databook*, Annual Issues.
SOURCE: *Statistical Abstract of the U.S., 1991*, p. 102.

the fact that no medical school, even privately funded ones, charges a tuition as high as the true costs, so that state and federal dollars subsidize the actual costs of medical education) and ultimately raise costs of care. They raise costs of care because of an economic argument that, despite increased physician density, physicians have an unusually high ability to maintain their income levels by increasing the amount of care provided to patients or physician-generated demand and by increasing fees (Feldstein, 1970; Fuchs, 1978; Holahan, Hadley, Scanlon, & Lee, 1978). To the extent this is true, having too many physicians raises the overall costs of health care, creating a controversy as to the "best" number of physicians to be available.

A related controversy is that, for whatever reasons, from 1987 through 1990 the number of applicants to U.S. medical schools dropped, and this particularly caused a drop in the number of potential residents in internal medicine, family practice, and, to a lesser extent, pediatrics (Colwell, 1992). In 1991, 19% fewer U.S. medical school graduates entered residencies in these specialties than in 1986. In addition, actual applications to medical schools declined. Controversy exists as to why these declines have occurred. One consideration is that the primary care incomes have not kept up with specialty incomes and that the declines are a response to potential incomes (Colwell, 1992; Petersdorf, 1992). A different although related explanation is that specialists receive more professional and general respect and prestige, and this explains the lessening of interest in generalist care (Petersdorf, 1992).

Neither of these answers explains why medical school applications have declined in the past 5 years, although they were up slightly in fall 1991. Possible answers here are changing conditions of medical practice, with physicians being less dominant than in the past and having less autonomy and having to practice more in large groups and corporate settings. Related to this is the increasing importance of third party payors and even control over what procedures can be performed in which types of settings (Starr, 1982). The most controversial statement of this hypothesis is that of proletarianization, that physicians in the future will no longer be able to control the conditions of their work and will not be independent professionals, but highly trained technicians who perform their work at the behest of large corporate settings, with their actions dictated by nonprofessionals (McKinlay & Arches, 1985; McKinlay & Stoeckle, 1990).

Nursing and Supply of Personnel

Nursing is an occupation in a state of flux that often confuses the public. The old image is that of women and caring, a field that provides a good temporary career for women who marry, and an appropriate feminine role for those who do not (Reverby, 1990). The new image is unclear—at times that of an overly technical, career-oriented field and at other times that of submissive women, overworked and under the direction of doctors and administrators. One fact has changed little: Nurses are overwhelmingly women (more than 95%). One point of confusion is the multiple levels of nurses, particularly in hospital settings. The registered nurse (RN) usually has a 2- or 4-year college degree and the most advanced training, and can perform a wide variety of tasks. This may include coordinating the care of patients in the hospital under the orders of a physician. Licensed practical or vocational nurses (LPNs) typically have one year of training and perform a variety of tasks under the nominal supervision of RNs. Nurses' aides generally have on-the-job training and perform the menial tasks of patient care, many of which involve personal hygiene.

There are many controversies regarding nursing at present, but the most important one from a broader policy perspective is whether there is a nursing shortage. Two related ones are what the education of nurses ought to be and linkages between levels of nursing. Examining the issues of education and levels of nursing first, there have in the past 30 years been three routes of entry into becoming an RN. The traditional and declining route is that of hospital-based training, which often placed as much emphasis on provision of patient care services as it did on education (Moccia, 1990). The newest route is the 2-year associate degree program through a community college. This route now produces twice as many graduates each year as do 4-year baccalaureate degree programs. There continue to be proposals that all new RNs have a bachelor's degree, but so far the leadership of 4-year nursing schools has not been able to achieve this goal. Although it is increasingly true that the positions with the most professional advancement are open mainly to 4-year graduates, many starting positions pay very similarly across all three types of education, and many hospital staff jobs do not differentiate between types of training, nor does state licensure.

In addition to the three levels of RNs, there is an issue of the relative situation of LPNs and aides. One critical issue here, particularly for

LPNs, is whether there is an easy route of advancement for skilled LPNs. In the past, there were limited options, but many associate programs now have special tracks to aid LPNs to upgrade to an associate degree RN. Many baccalaureate programs are also adding special routes to a 4-year B.S. degree for 2-year graduates, but these are not available everywhere, creating difficulties for career advancement.

How well are nurses paid? Nurses are not well paid relative to their level of training, and relative to physicians. At the end of World War II, RNs earned one-third of physicians' incomes, whereas now they earn about one-fifth. Relative to other female-dominated fields, the differentials are less clear. Until recently, nurses generally earned less than public school teachers in most areas, and yet had less-attractive working conditions and schedules. In some of the largest metropolitan areas, however, starting nursing salaries have increased to the $35,000 to $40,000 level, above that of starting public school teachers.

Is there a nursing shortage? One paradox today is the reality of more and more nurses and yet still a shortage (Moccia, 1990; Moscovice, 1988; Newschaffer & Schoeman, 1990). While the perception of nursing shortages in the past has often been cyclical, with cycles of too few nurses, some improvements in salary and additional recruits into the field, stability in numbers or an oversupply, stagnation of salaries, and then gradual perceptions of a shortage again, the situation the past 5 years appears to be shifting. There were clear shortages in 1979-1980 and 1986-1988, relative to number of positions to be filled, even if the absolute numbers of nurses available were high (Newschaffer & Schoeman, 1990). As Table 6.1 indicates, both the absolute number of nurses and the rate per 100,000 population had been increasing from 1970 to 1988. By 1985 there were more nurses (both RNs and LPNs) than ever before, a higher labor force participation rate among RNs than in any other period (more than 80%), and more working in hospitals than ever in recent history (more than 68%), yet the perception of a shortage, particularly in the hospital sector (Moccia, 1990). One argument has been that nurses do not remain in the same positions for long, creating a perception of continued shortages. Recent data from the American Hospital Association's Center for Nursing is shown in Figure 6.1 and illustrates that nurses are fairly stable in length of employment, with almost half having been at their current hospital for more than 5 years.

One controversy is whether there continues to be a shortage, one which will become worse in future years as more and more technology leads to the need for more nurses while few women (and even fewer

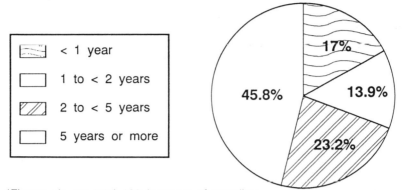

*Figures do not total 100 because of rounding

Figure 6.1. Length of Employment for Full-Time RNs, by Percent of Hospital's Total Work Force (April 1989)

SOURCE: Reprinted from *AHA News,* Vol. 27, No. 27, p. 4, by permission, July 8, 1991, Copyright 1991, American Hospital Publishing, Inc.

men) enroll in nursing programs, or whether we are coming out of another cycle and numbers of new entrants into nursing are again increasing. Some argue that numbers of nursing enrollments are up (Mayer, 1991; Newschaffer & Schoeman, 1990; "Nursing school enrollments up," 1992). Others argue that the availability of alternative careers for women, and especially alternative careers within medicine, will lead to a continued problem of nursing shortages (Delevan & Koff, 1990). Many of these critics argue that changing salary structures, and especially the issue of salary compression, may help to overcome recurrent shortages.

Allied Health Fields

A more difficult issue than coordination and career advancement within professional (registered) nursing and other levels of nursing are the same issues within the allied health fields. At least two quite different groups are involved here, beyond the non-RN levels of nurses already discussed. One is the group of technologists and technicians. The other is a group of new occupations, such as nurse practitioners and physicians' assistants, and a proposal by the American Medical Association

(AMA) to create a new category of health care worker, the RCT, registered care technician. Technologists and technicians have had the most rapid growth in the past 30 years. A critical issue here is the lack of any structured job mobility. Typically, entrants are narrowly trained for one specific technical field, with reasonable starting salaries but few advancements (Aries & Kennedy, 1990). Many people are attracted to the field initially because of reasonable pay and high job security, but become disillusioned over time and leave. No stepped routes to mid-level positions have been created. In fact, these fields have very little independence and few options for change. With the exception of nursing, the professional associations of allied health workers are controlled by the Committee on Education, creating major questions as to whether there are many easy options of change.

Several other special fields are mid-level health professionals, such as nurse practitioners (NPs) and physicians' assistants (PAs), and the AMA's recently proposed new type of health care worker. Both PAs and NPs were created to deal with a perceived physician shortage. Given declines in physician shortages, many experts feel that NP and PA roles will decline, although the growth of large group practices, such as in managed care, has kept a work setting open to many.

In June 1988 the AMA created a huge controversy by proposing a new category of bedside caregiver, the registered care technologist (RCT). This was the AMA's solution to the nursing shortage and it brought an immediate outcry from the American Nurses Association and most nurses (Alspach, 1989; Provencher, 1989). The AMA proposed three levels of training: 2-, 9-, and 18-month programs. Nursing viewed these new workers as a direct threat. Two years later, the AMA dropped the idea, stating that just the suggestion had brought enough attention to the shortage of caregivers ("Claiming success," 1990). The controversy may continue, however, since in 1991 the AMA continued to circulate a letter to hospitals, suggesting new programs of care attendants with 2 months' training, and care technicians with 7 months' training ("AMA still pushing," 1991).

Settings of Care

Thus far this chapter has reviewed current issues and controversies among the people who provide health care. Much of the rest of this chapter will focus upon similar background data and current controversies about where care is provided (sites) rather than who provides the care. We will first explore ambulatory or outpatient care very briefly, and then focus upon hospital-based care.

Ambulatory Care, Managed Care, and HMOs

One of the major growth areas in health care today is ambulatory care. More and more services are being provided in that setting, such as outpatient surgery and advanced types of diagnostic procedures. While traditionally ambulatory care was care delivered in doctor's offices, or a few outpatient settings such as hospital clinics, today the site of such care is more varied and can include special facilities for outpatient surgeries, emergency care, walk-in clinics, and group care settings such as health maintenance organizations (HMOs), in addition to the more traditional doctor's office. Health maintenance organizations typically refer to a combination of the provision of health care services along with an insurance function. The older type of HMO would be a plan, such as Kaiser, that provides care in group settings, may run its own hospitals, and is the insurance plan in that it is the group to which premiums are paid. Such plans usually cover almost all health care services, with minimal fees at the time a patient receives care, such as a $5 or $10 copayment for a doctor visit or a prescription. Newer types of provisions include IPAs (individual practice associations) in which the insurance plan contracts with a number of different providers to give care, often at their own office location. One idea behind such plans is to create an incentive to keep the patient well (hence the name *health maintenance* organization) by having the plan financially at risk for most care. This should create greater emphasis on preventive care and on finding problems at an early stage and treating them when they are smaller.

Although the older HMOs such as Kaiser were nonprofit, much of the growth of HMOs in the past 20 years has been through for-profit HMOs (Kronenfeld & Whicker, 1990). The most rapidly growing segment of the managed care market is the insurer-owned managed care plan (Hoy, Curtis, & Rice, 1991). In 1990 managed care plans comprised 25% of the market for members of the Health Insurance Association of America, up from only 1% in 1982 (Hoy et al., 1991). Almost

40% of all employees nationwide are now receiving health care through such plans. One fear and controversy is whether economic incentives may be too strong and lead to undertreatment of conditions. Moreover, running HMOs at a profit has been a problem for many companies, with such major corporations as Humana cutting back sharply because of economic losses (Kenkel, 1988). Maxicare had more than 2 million members in 1986 and was touted as the best managed HMO in the industry. It filed for bankruptcy protection 3 years later (Christianson, Wholey, & Sanchez, 1991). Some companies, such as Cigna, have been successful both with number of enrollees and profits.

A number of health reform plans envision a model of competing HMOs as one way to reorganize the health care system to provide more comprehensive care to most patients and yet control costs. But these approaches to reform do not always reflect the reality of patient experiences in managed care. One reason that more HMOs are profitable now than a few years ago is that rates have dramatically increased, raising questions as to the extent to which provision of care in the HMO setting would actually contain costs if such settings were more widely spread across the United States. Given the problems created when Maxicare and other plans have gone bankrupt, many state are enacting legislation to more closely regulate the plans and to increase financial assets required to operate as an HMO (Christensen et al., 1991). Such regulations will slow growth but, it is hoped, provide more adequate protection to consumers in the future. Whether managed care is the "wave of the future" and the solution to reform of the health care system remains to be proven.

Hospitals

Hospitals have played an important role in the delivery of health care services in the United States for at least the past 60 years and perhaps as far back as 1900. Up to now, the modern hospital, especially in the post-World War II era, has been the key resource and organizational hub of the U.S. health care system. It has been central to delivery of patient care, training of personnel, and conduct and dissemination of health-related research (Haglund & Dowling, 1988). Hospitals are important both in the total amount of health care delivered and as a major employment sector. They are the second- or third-largest industry in the United

States in terms of numbers of people employed and they employ about three-quarters of all the health care workers. About 40% of total health care expenses go to the hospital sector, and close to 60% of all federal expenditures on health services go to hospitals. Whether hospitals will remain the key resource and organizational hub of the health care system is one of the controversial questions about the organization and structure of the health care delivery system in the twenty-first century. However, a brief review of hospital history and current structure is necessary to be able to discuss current controversial issues.

History and Current Structure

The history of hospitals is long, but not in the versions we think of today (Rosenberg, 1987; Stevens, 1989). The early origins of the hospital trace back to almshouses, poorhouses, and workhouses established by city and county government to care for the poor, with almshouses evolving as the specialized institution to care for the sick poor (Rosenberg, 1987). In the late 1700s and early 1800s, some voluntary hospitals began to emerge, often at the urging of physicians who wanted places in which to practice surgery in the manner in which they had been taught in Europe. By the late 1800s the growth of modern science, the germ theory of disease and control of infections through aseptic technique, as well as the application of anesthesia into surgery, all combined with more general societal trends of industrialization and urbanization to create a more important role for hospitals as the providers of care not just to the poor but also to a growing middle class, and even to the wealthy (Rosenberg, 1987).

There have really been two traditions of hospital services in the United States: the private sector, partially nonprofit and particularly so after World War II, and the public sector (Kronenfeld & Whicker, 1984). Hospital care for the poor was concentrated in county or municipal hospitals until the introduction in 1965 of the Medicaid program to provide health care for the poor. The private sector consisted of voluntary, nonprofit hospitals, including typical community hospitals, those affiliated with religious associations, and other types of nonprofit hospitals (Stevens, 1989). At the turn of the century, most for-profit hospitals were run by physicians and were often set up in smaller communities and rural communities to provide an individual doctor or a few doctors in town a place in which to practice. Half of the hospitals in the United States were for-profit in 1900. This proportion decreased over the twentieth century, so that by 1970 only 13% of hospitals were for-profit (Kronenfeld & Whicker, 1984).

How hospital care has been paid for since 1920 is very important in understanding the major policy issues today. Up until World War II, most hospital care for middle-class people was paid for through savings. The Depression caused major problems for hospital incomes, both because people could not pay for care and because charitable donations for care of the poor were down. The financial solvency of many hospitals was threatened. Hospitals came up with the idea of voluntary group hospitalization plans, especially through Blue Cross (Haglund & Dowling, 1988; Stevens, 1989). Private insurance for hospital care grew rapidly, so that by 1965 most of the working population had third party insurance to cover most of the costs of a hospital stay. With the introduction of Medicare for the elderly and Medicaid for the poor in 1965, significant groups of people who did not previously have money or insurance to pay for care received that option.

The growth of private insurance and the two governmental programs initially provided enormous revenues for hospitals in the United States. The public plans and private insurance together ensured the financial stability of hospitals and increased the demand for such services. In fact, since many people had coverage for hospital care but not doctor or outpatient care, in the 1960s and 1970s, demand for hospital care was quite high, even for services that probably could have been performed outside the hospital. One study examining hospital admissions from 1974 to 1982 found that 23% of admissions studies were inappropriate and 17% could have been avoided through the use of outpatient surgery (Siu, Sonnenberg, & Manning, 1986).

Hospitals enjoyed a period of growth and prosperity. The actual number of hospitals declined slightly from 1971 to 1988, however, as Table 6.2 shows. Much of this decline was due to a decrease in the number of governmental hospitals, while the numbers of nonprofit hospitals declined slightly and the numbers of for-profit hospitals actually increased from 1971 to 1990. One other important trend in this period was the decline in hospitals with a smaller number of beds.

Payment for Hospitals

The method of reimbursement used by most private insurers and initially by Medicare, cost-based reimbursement, led to high hospital costs. In this system, hospitals simply pass along all the costs of

Table 6.2 Hospitals and Nursing Homes—Summary Characteristics: 1971 to 1988 (Except as indicated, based on National Master Facility Inventory)

Year & Type of Facility	Total	Facilities Under			Facilities With			Residents[2] (1,000)	Full-time employees (1,000)
		Govt. control	Proprietary control	Nonprofit control	Fewer than 24 beds[1]	25-74 beds	75 or more beds		
1971: All facilities	29,682	4,178	18,091	7,413	8,902	10,959	9,821	2,262	3,007
Nursing homes	22,004	1,368	17,049	3,587	8,266	8,259	5,479	1,076	568
Hospitals	7,678	2,810	1,042	3,826	636	2,700	4,342	1,186	2,439
1980: All facilities	30,116	3,498	19,611	7,007	8,852	8,573	12,691	2,427	3,919
Nursing homes[3][4]	23,065	936	18,669	3,460	8,498	6,362	8,205	1,396	798
Hospitals	7,051	2,562	942	3,547	354	2,211	4,486	1,031	3,121
1986: All facilities[6]	32,600	3,275	21,399	7,926	9,903	8,755	13,942	2,427	(NA)
All hospitals[6]	6,954	2,230	1,176	3,548	290	2,150	4,514	874	3,241
General	5,956	1,871	829	3,256	259	1,849	3,848	690	2,871
Psychiatric	584	267	218	99	12	140	432	139	248
Chronic	44	30	4	10	—	6	38	13	21
Tuberculosis	4	3	—	1	—	1	3	—	1
Nursing homes[4]	25,646	1,045	20,223	4,378	9,513	6,605	9,428	1,553	(NA)
1987: All hospitals[6]	6,940	2,220	1,216	3,504	314	2,155	4,471	865	3,318
General	5,880	1,858	815	3,207	281	1,817	3,782	683	2,943
Psychiatric	637	270	267	100	14	165	458	138	255
Chronic	41	30	4	7	—	5	36	12	20
Tuberculosis	5	4	—	1	—	1	4	—	1
1988: All hospitals[5,6]	6,927	2,210	1,228	3,489	308	2,175	4,444	859	3,349
General	5,795	1,852	764	3,179	275	1,793	3,727	680	2,973
Psychiatric	696	268	319	109	16	201	479	137	260
Chronic	42	33	1	8	—	5	37	13	17
Tuberculosis	4	3	—	—	—	1	3	—	1

— Represents or rounds to zero. NA Not available. [1] For hospitals, minimum of 6 beds; for nursing homes, minimum of 3 beds. [2] Number of residents as of date of interview. [3] Includes 1978 data for Alaska and South Dakota. [4] Excludes hospital based nursing homes; 1986 data based on the 1986 Inventory of Long—Term Care Places. Data may not be strictly comparable with previous year data. [5] Estimated. [6] Includes types not shown below. Based on data from the American Hospital Association.
SOURCE: National Center for Health Statistics, *Health Resources Statistics*, 1971 and *Statistical Abstract of the U.S.*, 1991, p. 105.

providing services directly to the third party payor. There is no incentive for the hospital to contain costs, leading to rapidly rising hospital costs in the late 1960s and 1970s. A number of strategies have been used to try to control rising hospital costs. These include regulations to limit new equipment and facilities, federally mandated price freezes, and business coalitions. The issues of costs of health care are explored in more detail in the next chapter.

One critical issue for hospitals was the passage in 1982 of the diagnosis related groups (DRG) reimbursement system as part of the Tax Equity and Fiscal Responsibility Act of 1982. This converted the way Medicare paid for hospital care from a cost-based reimbursement system to a prospective per case system based on the diagnosis of the patient, with more than 460 different diagnostic-related payment categories. Instead of a hospital being able to charge a patient a set fee per day plus specific charges for supplies and other special facilities, the hospital care of Medicare patients is now paid with one fee set in advance, based on the expected average length of stay and services used. Many states now also reimburse the hospital stays of Medicaid patients with the same approach. Thus whereas before hospitals could almost be certain of breaking even or having excess revenues on the care of every patient, except for charity cases or bad debts (where no one paid), they must now figure out how to provide care at the preset fees provided by Medicare (and in some states, Medicaid). Since elderly people use the most hospital care, this reimbursement change affects half or more of most hospital stays. How to break even on care provision has suddenly become a major issue for hospitals. Moreover, this new policy has an explicit assumption that hospitals are businesses in competition with one another and with different categories of patients. The federal DRG system for Medicare patients provides a common set of operating procedures and detailed regulations to ensure care for one set of patients, those on Medicare (Stevens, 1989). Hospitals must now figure out how to provide care and not lose money on all patients, including Medicare, under several different reimbursement systems. Thus managing a hospital has shifted from being a situation in which a manager was almost sure to be successful to being one of trying to maximize the types of patients and revenue they represent at any given time, while still keeping the hospital staff (and the community, in the case of nonprofit community facilities) reasonably satisfied.

Current Policy Issues in Hospitals

What are the major policy issues and controversies surrounding hospital care today? Some of them link to the issues just discussed of financing, how hospitals can finance new facilities, and how hospitals can be profitable in a new era. Other controversies relate to ownership of hospitals and the extent to which for-profit hospital chains are a good idea, and whether the role of hospitals in the health care system is changing.

For-Profit Hospitals

The for-profit sector of health care grew rapidly in the 1970s, after a decade-long decline. As compared to for-profit facilities at the turn of the century, most of the new for-profit hospitals are part of investor-owned hospital chains. One important sector of these hospitals is psychiatric, with very different trends of costs, use, and policy issues. In general health care, hospitals in the for-profit sector are concentrated in the Sunbelt (southern and southwestern) states and in California. Within any given sector of the country, for-profits are more likely to be located in suburban areas (Kronenfeld & Whicker, 1990). There has been much concern about the growth of for-profit hospitals and whether they will harm the economic solvency of other types of hospitals. Other concerns are that they do not provide charity care and may provide a different quality of care (Gray, 1986).

One hotly debated question is whether for-profit ownership has an impact on the cost of care. Some experts argue that for-profit hospitals increase total health care costs both by exploiting any inadequacies in the system of paying for care and by earning higher dollars for a similar procedure than would a different facility. Others argue that the general business know-how of private sector management may be applied in the for-profit sector and allow those hospitals to provide care more efficiently. Most studies to explore this issue arrive at inconclusive results as to whether costs in such facilities are higher or the same as in nonprofit facilities (Kronenfeld & Whicker, 1984).

Two other questions about the growth of for-profits is whether they limit access to care and whether they provide poor-quality care. There appear to be few quality differences between types of hospitals, at least based on generally used measures of quality. For-profit hospitals do discourage admission of uninsured patients, but increasingly all hospitals except for publicly funded facilities do so. Not-for-profit hospitals do appear to provide somewhat more uncompensated and charity care, although because those facilities are tax exempt, one could argue that they have a greater obligation to provide charity care (Kronenfeld & Whicker, 1984). A major report by the Institute of Medicine in 1986 concluded that the differences between for-profit and not-for-profit health care organizations do not justify recommending that such ownership be supported or opposed as a public policy issue (Gray, 1986). This conclusion still appears appropriate.

Financing Issues and the Economic Health of Hospitals

There are often two or more ways of considering many issues. This is particularly true when we examine the issue of costs of hospital care. In the next chapter, we will look at costs partly from a perspective of the total society and the governmental sector. From that perspective, controlling the amount of dollars spent on hospital care is good. From the perspective of a hospital administrator, however, any decrease in dollars spent on health care raises questions of how hospitals of the future will pay their bills. The whole intent of the shift to DRG-based payment for hospital services for Medicare patients was to slow the rate of increase in government expenses for hospital care, both by holding down the costs of each specific hospitalization and possibly by lowering the numbers of admissions, since new peer review organizations were also set up to monitor inpatient care for appropriateness of treatment. Most experts now agree that the changes in Medicare did slow significantly the spending for hospital inpatient care (Christensen, 1991). Also, admission rates declined from 1983 through 1987, and rates in 1989 for people 65 and over were still only 85% of rates in 1983 (Christensen, 1991). Overall occupancy rates have also declined, and there has been a wave of hospital closures, mostly inner-city and rural hospitals.

What do we conclude from these figures? Part of the controversy over hospital costs and financing is that, as a nation, we want more and more care but do not want to pay for it. While the overall annual rate of inflation for hospital care has declined from a high of almost 15% in 1982 before a number of federal legislative changes, hospital costs continue to increase at rates above the cost of living. If costs continue to rise (and the earlier part of this chapter presented some reasons, such as pressure to increase the pay of health care personnel, that will keep costs up) and certain programs such as Medicare and Medicaid hold down the amount they pay, then the costs charged to other patients will go up even faster. This is known as cost shifting, or increasing the costs of care to payors without limits to make up deficiencies in costs for other patients. This strategy has a limited utility, because in many cities major employers and insurers now bargain with hospitals for discounted rates for their employees. At some point there will be few other patient groups onto whom hospitals can shift the full costs of care. Most experts now agree that hospitals are run more efficiently than previously, and such areas as purchasing have been overhauled in an effort to cut the costs of supplies. Many of the most basic issues in hospitals relate to overall financing of health care, issues to be explored in greater depth in the next chapter and the last chapter of this book.

One specialized controversial issue in hospitals is how to pay for new physical facilities and equipment. Traditionally, community-based hospitals used fund drives to raise money for new equipment. The Hill-Burton legislation passed in the late 1940s provided an infusion of capital funds to hospitals and led to many new buildings and much new equipment through the 1950s and 1960s. As these funds disappeared, many nonprofit hospitals turned to tax-exempt bonds, and the for-profit hospitals relied on general corporate revenues. By 1984 debt was the source of 76% of hospital capital financing. The United States is almost unique among countries in financing hospital construction in this way. In most countries that have national health care systems and governmentally owned hospitals, capital costs are met from governmental revenues and appropriations. The growth in debt has been a major reason for the financial problems of some for-profit hospital chains and also a major problem for nonprofit hospitals. One solution for purchasing new equipment has been joint ventures between hospitals and physicians, in which the physician groups provide long-term capital and credit while sharing in the use of the facilities and any potential profits. This has worked for equipment with high profit potential, but not for typical capital needs. A continuing controversy with Medicare and Medicaid is to what extent capital funds also be provided. Some private insurers are also raising this issue. The overriding importance of financial incentives in hospitals today has shifted power in health care from providers such as hospitals to organizations that pay for care, including private health insurance companies and government. This controversy over how much to pay for hospital care and how to pay for capital expenses will likely continue until the United States reaches some greater consensus on health care system reform.

The Changing Hospital Role

It may be that hospitals are losing their dominance over health care. More and more procedures and surgery are now done in outpatient settings. Third party payors, such as insurance companies, are able to dictate terms of treatment. More after-hospital care is now being provided in patients' homes and long-term care facilities, as a way to hold down costs and maximize the revenues from DRG-based payments by shifting the patient from the hospital to other care settings. There is now great controversy and ambiguity over the future role of hospitals. Hospitals in the United States have long represented values of science and have carried important cultural weight for that reason. They have also represented charity and caring, particularly in the nonprofit sector, both religiously and non-religiously based. Earlier in the century they also represented forces for social order. All of these values are shifting, with a greater emphasis on hospitals as businesses. Moreover, more and more advanced care is now occurring outside of hospitals. Will they become only a collection of specialized workshops? Will the notion of the hospital extend beyond the walls of the institution to the application of medical care technology in a wide variety of service settings, with the hospital basically becoming the health care system? A major expert on hospitals, Stevens (1989), concludes that hospitals in the United States are in flux. She argues that we have a de facto national health system through our hospitals, but are unwilling to recognize the fact, and that "while the American hospital industry has major deficiencies as a public service, as a largely private industry it has been enormously successful" (pp. 352-353). The future is far less clear.

Special Problems of Rural Settings

One underlying assumption of much federal health personnel and institutional policy in the 1960s and early 1970s was that increasing the overall supply of physicians and hospitals would help to improve the geographic distribution. In reality, this improvement has not occurred. Despite increases in the number of physicians in the United States, such that the physician-to-population ratio decreased from one physician per 840 in 1960 to one per 524 in 1983, most of this improvement occurred in urban and suburban areas. Rural counties with the smallest populations have gained the fewest new physicians (Moscovice, 1988).

A number of special programs and policies have been implemented to try to increase the supply of physicians (and other health personnel) in rural areas. These include special programs of loan forgiveness, location of physicians in rural areas through the National Health Service Corps, the development of area health education centers, and specialized medical education programs to preferentially admit a certain number of rural students into medical school and to return some of the students to clinical training in the rural areas. Few of these efforts have yielded substantial and lasting results. Studies of why physicians do not locate in rural areas reveal such reasons as lack of adequate medical facilities; professional isolation; limited support services; lack of social, cultural, and educational opportunities for the entire family; and lack of employment opportunities for the spouse (Rosenblatt & Moscovice, 1982). Controversy continues as to what policies might play a role in solving this problem of insufficient rural physicians. The idea of simply overproducing physicians, such that some eventually locate in rural areas, appears both inefficient and nonproductive.

Attraction of physicians and retention of hospitals are related issues. Hospitals cannot stay open in rural areas if no physicians are available to staff them, and few physicians wish to move to an area without a hospital available. There are special problems of rural hospitals, however. Most rural hospitals are small (fewer than 100 beds), and small facilities such as this are becoming less viable economically. Labor requirements are high and occupancy rates are often low, making such hospitals less efficient to operate (Haglund & Dowling, 1988). Rural hospital occupancy rates had declined as low as 52% in 1984, and for the one in three rural hospitals with fewer than 50 beds, the occupancy rate was only 40% (Ermann, 1990). As technological demands increase, it is more and more difficult for small facilities to compete. In addition, there is evidence that rural patients often prefer to be in urban hospitals, viewing care there as of higher quality, and will bypass smaller facilities for regional centers (U.S. Congress, 1988). This is particularly true of rural patients with insurance, which often leaves the rural hospital with patients who are unable to pay for care. Related to this is some evidence that the closure of rural hospitals is linked with declining economic bases in the surrounding rural community, raising more basic questions of economic policy rather than of health care policy (Probst, Kronenfeld, Amidon, & Hussey, 1992).

Controversy exists over the best way to maintain some adequate level of health resources in rural areas. Regionalization and networking may be required. Examples would include small communities jointly sponsoring one larger facility and having small overnight stay hospitals and emergency facilities available in rural areas, with routine approaches to transfer patients to larger, better equipped facilities as soon as they are stabilized. Moreover, the health care problems of rural areas may be inseparable from larger issues of overall economics and the declining viability of these communities.

7

Costs of Health Care

This chapter focuses on costs of health care, the first of three chapters examining the three big issues of health services research: cost, quality, and access. Obviously, all three are interrelated, but this chapter will try to maintain a focus on how many dollars we are spending for health care, how those have been changing over time, and what the major efforts have been to control rising costs of health care services.

One important factor to remember about how much health care costs in the United States and how we finance or pay for care is that the system for financing health care in the United States is not really a unified system. We can present national data, but financing of health care services reflects the fragmentation in the U.S. system as a whole. What we find is a patchwork of poorly connected financing mechanisms, with variance by patient type, type of provider, and type of service.

One useful approach of some analysts of our health care financing system is to talk of four categories of expenses: how much money is spent, where the money comes from (direct out-of-pocket, private insurance, government), what it is spent on (fees paid to individual providers, to hospitals, for drugs or medically related supplies), and how it is paid out to the providers (per unit of service, per item of care, per hospital discharge, per day of long-term care services) (Jonas, 1992). Although the following discussion will not adhere strictly to those categorizations, they present a useful way to summarize one aspect of financing health care services.

Trends in Health Care Expenditures

Proportion of GNP and Aggregate Costs

National health care expenditures have grown at a rate substantially outpacing the gross national product since 1940. Prior to World War II, only 4% of the GNP was spent on health care. By 1960, this figure had increased only to 5.3%. Expressed in per capita terms, the growth in health expenditures appears much larger, partially because this was a period of rapid economic growth. Per capita expenses increased from $30 per capita in 1940 to $146 in 1960 (Waldo, Levit, & Lazerby, 1986). These trends continued and accelerated in the next 20 years, as the percent of gross national product spent on health care increased to 7.4% in 1970, and 9.4% in 1980. Per capita expenses also continued to increase, going from $350 a person in 1970 to $1,049 in 1980 in constant dollars (Waldo et al., 1986). These trends are illustrated in Figure 7.1.

These decade-long figures actually mask important trends occurring within each decade. Health expenditures as a percent of GNP were quite stable from 1950 to 1955, with more increase in the latter part of that decade (Kronenfeld & Whicker, 1984). Major impacts on expenditures were created by the passage of Medicare and Medicaid in 1965 and the beginning operation of those programs in 1966. A period of stabilization of prices occurred from 1971 to 1973 because the federal government had wage and price controls in place due to the Economic Stabilization Program (ESP) (Levit, Lazerby, Letsch, & Cowan, 1991a). After the lifting of all ESP controls and the expansion of the Medicare program to more completely include the disabled, costs rose by 1976 to 8.5% of GNP. Then a voluntary effort to hold down health care costs ensued from 1976 through 1979 but gradually lost its effectiveness.

What happened to health care expenditures during the decade of the '80s? Cost pressures continued to build overall, despite various efforts to control spending and hold down costs in certain sectors, such as the passage of the DRG-based payment system for Medicare hospital expenses in the early 1980s. Spending for health care continued to grow by almost all measures, with particular acceleration since 1986 (Lazerby

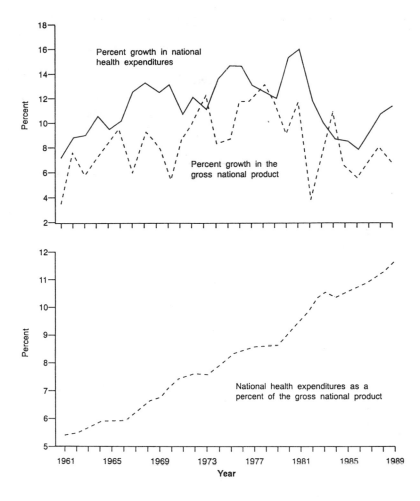

Figure 7.1. Percent Growth in National Health Expenditures and Gross National Product, and National Health Expenditures as a Percent of Gross National Product: Calendar Years 1961-1989

SOURCE: *Health Care Financing Review,* Winter 1990, Volume 12, p. 3.

& Letsch, 1990). By 1990 health care expenditures reached $666.2 billion, up to 12.2% of the gross national product, an increase of 10.5% from 1989 to 1990. This is an inflation rate substantially greater than the increase in overall GNP. In fact, the increase in the share of GNP spent for health care from 1989 to 1990 is the second-largest such jump since 1960. The percent of the GNP being expended on health care had increased to 10.7% in 1985, 11.6% in 1989, and 12.2% in 1990 (Levit, Lazerby, Cowan, & Letsch, 1991b). One explanation for the large jump is the slowdown in the general economy. Percent of GNP spent on health is very sensitive to overall economic growth because the denominator figure in percent of GNP spent on health is a measure of overall output of the economy. The trends on per capita expenditure are less dependent on overall economic trends. Per capita expenditures also continued to increase, up to $2,354 per capita in 1989 and $2,566 in 1990. This was an increase of 9.4% in one year. Of these per capita expenditures, public funds account for $1,089 per capita (42.4% of the total expenditures for health care) and private funds paid for the remaining $1,478 (57.6%) (Levit et al., 1991b).

Trends in Types of Health Care Expenditures and Sources of Funds

Figure 7.2 shows where the nation's health dollars both came from and went in 1960 and 1990. This allows a comparison of types of sources of revenue and expenditure over time, before beginning a more detailed examination first of types of health care expenditures and then sources of revenue. A comparison of the sources of funds between 1960 and 1990 shows the greater influence of the role of government by 1990. Only 24 cents out of every health dollar in 1960 went to government programs. By 1990, government programs of all types accounted for 42 cents out of each health dollar—17 cents for Medicare, 11 for Medicaid (neither of which existed as a separate program in 1960) and the rest for other types of government programs both at the federal level and at state and local levels. The next-largest source of the health care dollar in 1990 was private health insurance, which covered 33 cents. In 1960 private health insurance covered only 22 cents of each dollar. Far and away the largest source of the health care dollar in 1960 was out-of-pocket payments (that is, costs not reimbursed to the consumer). This category was 49 cents, or almost half of all the health care dollar in 1960, but was only 20 cents by 1990.

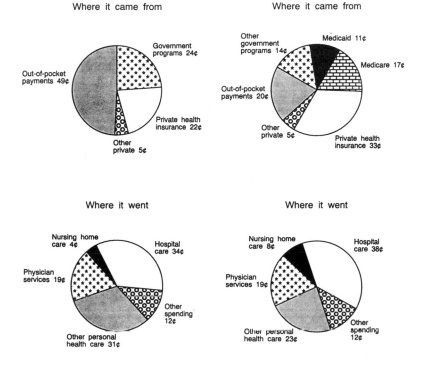

Figure 7.2. The Nation's Health Dollar, 1960 and 1990

SOURCE: Health Care Financing Administration, Office of the Actuary: Data From the Office of National Cost Estimates.

NOTES: *Other private* includes industrial in plant health services, non-patient revenues, and privately financed construction. *Other personal health care* includes dental, other professional services, home health care, drugs and other non-durable medical products, and vision products and other durable medical products. *Other spending* covers program administration and the net cost of private health insurance, government public health, and research and construction.

A comparison of where the health care dollar actually went in 1960 and 1990 reveals much greater similarities over the 30 years. Hospital care was the largest single category of expense at both times and took up 34 cents of the health care dollar in 1960 and 38 cents in 1990. The catch-all category of other personal health care, which includes such diverse services as dental, drugs, home health, and vision care, was the next-largest single category in both years and was higher in 1960 (31 cents) than in 1990 (23 cents). Physician services took 19 cents of the health expenditure dollar at both time periods. Nursing home care is one category that has doubled, taking only 4 cents of the health care dollar in 1960 but 8 cents in 1990 (Levit et al., 1991b; Office of National Cost Estimates, 1990).

Personal health care expenditures account for 87.9% of all national health expenditures, while supplies, research funds, and construction of medical care account for the rest of expenditures (Levit et al., 1991b). Personal health expenses have been increasing at rates higher than the cost of living over the past 30 years.

Why have the costs of health care been increasing so dramatically in the United States? The rates of growth have exceeded both the general inflation rate and rates explainable by simple population growth alone. Obviously the increase in the proportion of the population that is elderly is one factor and has already been explored in an earlier chapter. In general, there has been an increase in the rate of use of services per capita and in the intensity of services provided (Gibson & Waldo, 1981; Levit et al., 1991b). The implementation of Medicare and Medicaid did increase access for certain groups, and thus raised total expenditures. Additional factors that have contributed to increased costs are favorable attitudes toward the use of new medical technology and increased availability of health insurance (Kronenfeld & Whicker, 1984). Because more people have health insurance coverage, they are more likely to seek out care. Additionally, in the past some physicians and hospitals provided charity care to those without insurance, and the cost of this care did not go into national expenditure figures.

Technology raises total health expenditures by creating types of services that did not even exist in the past. Costs particularly go up in the case of half-way technology, where medicine is able to help control a disease but not cure it (Fuchs, 1974). One of the best examples of the interaction of new technology and coverage for care has occurred in the treatment of kidney disease. Before the development of kidney dialysis, patients whose kidneys no longer functioned died in a short period of time. The dialysis machines circulate the patient's blood through an artificial kidney located outside the body, removing toxic wastes and excess fluids. A typical regimen of therapy would last for 3 to 6 hours at a time, often three times a week. Since 1973 patients with this disease have been eligible for Medicare coverage. The annual cost of this

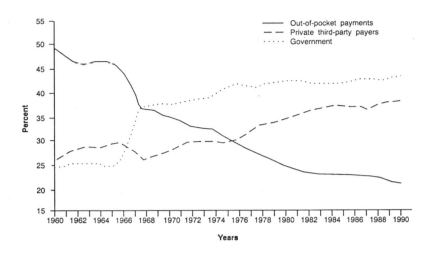

Figure 7.3. Distribution of National Health Expenditures by Source of Financing: 1960-1990

SOURCE: Health Care Financing Administration, *Health Care Financing Review,* Fall 1991, v. 13, p. 38.

treatment to the federal government is more than $2 billion a year for a disease affecting 70,000 patients (Kutner, 1982; Plough, 1986).

Have all types of health care expenditures been increasing at the same rate? In the past 30 years, spending for hospital care grew most rapidly in the 1960s and 1970s. From 1966 to 1983, the average annual rate of growth in hospital revenues was 14%. In 1984, after the implementation of the DRG system, the annual rate of growth in hospital care was cut in half, to 7%, demonstrating that hospital cost containment programs were somewhat effective. Hospital revenues began to increase again in the late 1980s, increasing 10.1% from 1989 to 1990. One shift in where hospital revenues come from is that public funds and insurance are paying more of the costs of hospital care, while the share of hospital care coming from out-of-pocket revenues has decreased from almost 21% in 1960 to only 5% currently (Levit et al., 1991b). In fact, out-of-pocket payments for total health expenditures have decreased from 50% of national health expenditures in 1960 to 20% in 1990, as shown in Figure 7.3. The role of government and third party payors has increased. Physician expenditures increased more rapidly in the decade of the '80s than did hospital care. More of this area of expenditure is now covered by insurance or government, with a little less than 20% of physician services now being paid out-of-pocket, versus 62% in 1960.

Most other areas of health expenditures are not as covered by insurance or government. In dental care, for example, more than half of all expenditures are still out-of-pocket. This is also true for prescription drug expenditures. Almost all expenditures for medical supplies, durable medical equipment, and over-the-counter medications are from out-of-pocket revenues. Vision products such as eyeglasses and contact lenses are the most important type of durable medical equipment (Levit et al., 1991b).

The most rapidly growing category of health care expenditures is for home health care. This category has grown particularly rapidly since 1988. In that year, Medicare clarified and expanded its home health care coverage. Public sources pay for almost three-quarters of all home health care, with more than half of that paid by Medicare (Levit et al., 1991b).

Costs Compared to Other Countries

Is this problem of rising health care costs unique to the United States? It is beyond the scope of this book and its focus on health care policy and controversies in the United States to examine this question in much depth. A few pertinent factors are important to consider, however. Some of the factors increasing health care costs (aging of the population, increased technology) are affecting many other countries. Even when similar trends are occurring, the impact on health care costs may not be the same. The United States has been much more likely to adopt new technology and spread it across the population (or the insured population) than have most other countries. One good example to compare across countries is kidney dialysis usage. The number of patients returning to full-time work after being placed on dialysis has actually decreased since the procedure became extensively covered and given to patients in worse overall health (Kutner, 1990). In contrast to making it a covered service for most of the population in the United States, Great Britain has many fewer machines and rarely provides this service to people over 65 unless their general health condition is exceptional. Most practitioners in Great Britain are comfortable with this decision and rarely discuss the possibility of alternatives with patients. Thus one controversy is whether we need to better control the use of technology or other high-cost features of our health care system.

Costs are much higher here than elsewhere, with per capita spending in this country 40% higher than that of Canada, and 65% greater than that of any European country (Schieber & Poullier, 1991). Moreover, the gap between the United States and other countries is growing (Rice, 1992). One reason other countries have been better able to control costs is because of the setup of their systems, which often incorporate total national health care expenditure limits.

Another important factor, which some critics argue is a partial explanation of why rising costs are a more serious problem in the United States than in other countries, relates to the deteriorating administrative efficiency of the U.S. health care system. In 1983 the proportion of health care expenditures devoted to administration was 60% higher in the United States than it was in Canada, and 97% higher than it was in Great Britain (Himmelstein & Woolhandler, 1986). Using 1987 data, one study has recently examined four components of administrative costs: insurance overhead, hospital administration, nursing home administration, and physicians' overhead and billing expenses (Woolhandler & Himmelstein, 1991). U.S. insurance companies retained more than $18 billion of their total premium revenues of $157.8 billion for overhead, 11.9% of premiums. The two government programs of Medicare and Medicaid retained $6.6 billion out of $207 billion in total costs, or 3.2% administrative costs. Added together, the total insurance administrative costs retained were 15.1% of the $500 billion spent for health care. In contrast, Canada's provincial plans retained only $235 million of the $26.5 billion spent, or less than 1% of administrative costs. The much smaller private insurance market in Canada reported administrative costs of 10.9% or $200 million of $1.83 billion, making the total Canadian insurance administrative costs 1.2% of health care spending. Thus U.S. insurance administrative costs were more than four times as high.

Differentials in other categories were smaller but still substantial (Woolhandler & Himmelstein, 1991). Hospital administrative costs and nursing home administrative costs were each about three times as high in Canada as in the United States. The comparisons on physician overhead cost are the least reliable, due to differences in basic data available. Overall, estimates are that 19% to 24% of total spending on health care in the United States is related to administrative costs, versus 8.4% to 11% in Canada.

Several factors explain the overall differentials, but one very important factor is the lessened efficiency of private insurance companies. The percent of premium devoted to overhead was similar for private insurance in each of the countries. Because so much more of the U.S. market is private, total insurance administrative costs are much higher. Moreover, comparing with their earlier work, Woolhandler and Himmelstein (1991) found that the U.S. administrative costs in 1987 were 37% higher than in 1983, despite the supposed increased attention to cost containment.

Administrative savings are not the only explanation of the differential costs in various countries. The government's monopoly power over provider payments and aspects of the system, such as technology diffusion, help to control costs in other countries (Rice, 1992). If the government provides the vast majority of health care payments, it has more power over the amount of money paid to individual providers. In fact, such trends of increased controls as a way to cut costs are currently under way in the Medicare and Medicaid programs. One expert argues that if the United States wants to control costs as other countries have, we may need to install some type of global budgeting with total limits for health care, a most controversial proposal in the United States (Glaser, 1986).

Major Policy Issues in the Cost Arena

The previous section has just demonstrated that the way in which health care is financed can have a major impact on total costs in the country. There are currently many proposals being discussed for reform of the U.S. health care system. All of these would impact costs of care and health care expenditures in various ways. A more detailed examination of the reform plans will be presented in the last chapter of this book, which will focus on access to health care and reform proposals. The policy issues and controversies we will explore in the rest of this chapter focus upon more specific types of proposals and changes that would alter some aspects of financing and delivery of health care, but not overall system reform.

Controlling Costs Within the Major Government Programs

The Impact of Medicare Reform

In the previous chapter, we reviewed studies which indicated that the DRG prospective hospital payment reform system, which was implemented by

Medicare in the early 1980s, did help to contain the growth in hospital costs to some extent. We also noted that the rate of growth in annual hospital expenses did slow for a few years after the implementation of the DRG system, but then the rate of growth again began to increase. Some of the early fears about the implementation of this system were that hospitals would discharge sick patients too quickly, which would lead to unnecessary readmissions. There was some evidence that this occurred during the early phases of the DRG payment system (Gay, Kronenfeld, Baker, & Amidon, 1989). Some reforms in payment of readmissions have been effected, so that readmissions within too short a period of time no longer generate the start of a new DRG payment for that hospitalization. Lengths of stay have dropped by about 0.9 days in 1984, and 0.6 days in 1985, compared to an average drop of 0.2 days per year from 1967 to 1983 (Koch, 1988). For the majority of patients, it no longer appears that access to needed care has lessened under DRG reimbursement (DesHarnais, Kobrinski, & Chesney, 1987).

There is evidence that under the DRG payment system, hospitals have shifted more care into outpatient settings. The revised payment approach applies only to inpatient care. One way that hospitals can continue to maximize revenues is through more outpatient admissions. One survey of physicians found that under PPS (Prospective Payment System), hospitals have encouraged more outpatient testing (Guterman & Dobson, 1986). A recent summary of the impact of the DRG system was that inpatient hospital care use declined initially and then stabilized from 1987 on, while outpatient hospital care continued to increase, as did costs for physician care (Edwards & Fisher, 1989). Thus the actual impact of the payment reform system on total costs has been less than hoped. As with so many reforms that affect only one payor and one type of services, there is much room for hospitals and other providers to learn how to "game" the system, that is, maximize revenue, given the new rules. Many analysts contend that piecemeal reforms of the health care system generally lead to disappointing results after a few years.

The other major area of reform within the Medicare program is a new physician payment approach. This new system is quite recent, having only begun in January 1992, thus the evaluative studies of the impact of the new system are not yet available. It has been a very controversial new policy. Physician groups launched protests in June 1992, when the initial draft regulations were first released. The AMA (American Medical Association) was so upset that it threatened to seek congressional action to change the proposed new system of reimbursement (McIlrath,

1991a). Physicians argued that the reimbursement scheme was not fair and that transition rules were particularly inappropriate (McIlrath, 1991b).

The new system proposes the use of a resource based relative value scale (RBRVS) initially developed by Hsiao (Hsiao, Yntema, Braun, & Becker, 1988). Previously, physicians had been paid on a basis of what their charges were for various services. In the studies prior to the development of the scales, how long it took physicians to perform various kinds of tasks was determined. Each service was assigned a relative weight, based on three geographically adjusted values for work, practice costs, and malpractice premiums. Thus the new payment schemes created were related to the time and resources used. For the final application, a scale of relative weightings or relative values was formed as the basis of the new physician reimbursement system for Medicare patients (Hsiao et al., 1988, 1990).

Based on the complaints in reaction to the initial drafts, the Health Care Financing Administration (HCFA) did revise the rules somewhat. Whereas the initial regulations would have increased slightly the fees paid to generalist physicians and decreased the specialist fees, negotiations with various groups from organized medicine, including the AMA, have been used as a basis for some modifications. It is now estimated that by 1996, payments for family physicians will increase by almost 30%, while payments for procedure-oriented specialties will drop by the same percentage (McIlrath, 1991c). Changes will be gradual from 1992 to 1996. If prior payments for a service were no more than 15% above or below the determined RBRVS rate, the service is moved immediately to the new payment system. If the gap is larger, initial year payments are a blend of RBRVS and the older historical payment system. In addition, the new system creates an incentive for physicians to be fully participating doctors who agree to accept the Medicare rate as payment in full in all cases. Those physicians will receive a full payment amount according to the schedule, while physicians who do not agree will receive only 95% of the scheduled amount (McIlrath, 1991d). The revised rules, issued in December 1991, will actually increase average payment levels in 16 states and four specialties, as compared to no states and one specialty in the June 1991 draft. Thus the protests by physicians have led to policy changes and some greater effort to seek cooperation with physicians (McIlrath, 1991d). Table 7.1 illustrates how the changes in Medicare payments will affect physicians in three different geographical locations.

Table 7.1 Location, Location, Location

Under Medicare's new national schedule, doctors in high-cost areas, like Manhattan and Miami, receive far less than what they customarily charge, while doctors in lower-cost areas, like Rochester, fare much better.
Here are the amounts doctors typically charge their patients under private insurance, the amounts doctors are allowed to charge under Medicare, and the portion that they can collect from Medicare.

Total Hip Joint Replacement

| | What the doctor charges for | | What |
	private patients	Medicare patients	Medicare pays
Manhattan	$5,881	$2,456	$2,068
Miami	4,237	2,181	1,837
Rochester	2,978	2,225	1,874

Office Visit

| | What the doctor charges for | | What |
	private patients	Medicare patients	Medicare pays
Manhattan	$110	$64	$54
Miami	71	58	49
Rochester	38-43	49	41

SOURCE: *The New York Times*, Sunday, April 12, 1992, p. 14. © 1992 by The New York Times Company. Reprinted by permission.

No one can yet predict how well the new RBRVS payment system will perform. Even if it does hold down cost increases, and in the long run shift the relative reimbursement of generalist physicians versus specialists, a shift in supply will take a long time to occur. This is because the pipeline between a person beginning to study medicine, choosing a residency and specialty, and then being in practice is at least 7 to 8 years, and often longer. Even then, the changes occur initially only in new graduates. Additionally, many in health care are concerned that a reimbursement change is also being used in an effort to impact the relative distribution of physicians, without adequate public discussion. Specifically, many physicians feel there has not been an adequate public or professional discussion of the issues involved. The implementation of RBRVS has led some physicians to argue that the health care system is becoming increasingly bureaucratic and is limiting the options for practice in the name of cost control. Controversy will continue about payment reforms and about the tension between holding down physician fees as a cost control measure and attracting young people into medicine, the issue of supply discussed in the previous chapter.

Controlling the Costs to States of the Medicaid Program

One of the major pushes behind health care reform from a state perspective is the growth in the Medicaid program. The overall issue of what should be done about Medicaid and how it might be modified in a reformed system will be discussed in Chapter 9. For this chapter on costs, however, it is helpful to appreciate the impact that rising medical care costs have had on state budgets. In addition, problems in paying for Medicaid are part of the problem of rising health care costs and uncovered health care costs (Fraser, Narcross, & Kralovec, 1991). Controversy abounds about Medicaid because of rapidly increasing costs, issues at times about quality of care, and its overall impact on state budgets and thus on state needs for tax and revenue increases, as well as on private insurance in the state.

How does Medicaid actually work? Coverage for the nation's poor is largely the responsibility of the Medicaid program, a joint federal/state entitlement program administered by states under broad federal guidelines. While many poor individuals are not covered by Medicaid, even the numbers currently covered (about 26 million people) are a major cost to state budgets. The federal government pays an average of 55% of the costs, a share that ranges from 50% to 80%, depending upon a state's per capita income (Pepper Commission, 1990). States set their own criteria for eligibility, typically in line with the state's eligibility for Aid to Families of Dependent Children, and extent of services within federal guidelines. Thus a family of three in California in 1990 was eligible for Medicaid with a monthly income of $934, 106% of the federal poverty level that year, while the same family in Alabama would be eligible for Medicaid only if its income was $118 or less.

Over the past several years, Congress has mandated coverage up to higher income levels for some groups. The major focus of expansion since 1984 has been for coverage for pregnant women and young children. The Omnibus Budget and Reconciliation Act of 1989 (OBRA, 1989) mandated that, beginning in April 1990, states had to cover pregnant women and children under age 6 with family incomes up to 133% of the federal poverty level. In addition, Congress mandated in

1988 that states had to continue Medicaid coverage for one year for beneficiaries who lose their eligibility for the program as their income increases. Both of these are worthwhile extensions from the perspective of access to care and improving health indicators. However, in many states, particularly those with less generous initial Medicaid coverage, the most rapidly increasing category of state expenditure has been the state match for the Medicaid program. A major concern in states has been the growth of what are called "entitlement" programs, typically joint federal/state programs where states do not control the number of people who become eligible but must come up with dollars to meet their share of expense. In addition to Medicaid, AFDC and unemployment insurance operate somewhat similarly. For Medicaid, however, the mandates have increased the costs of the program to states by expanding eligibility at the same time that costs of the actual medical services have also been increasing faster than general inflation and tax revenues, particularly during a recessionary economy. In some states, one of the largest single budget items is the Medicaid program. Medicaid has become a major controversy in a number of states, and this becomes one push for more general health care reform.

Additionally, another aspect of the problem with Medicaid and costs has been that as mandates have expanded, one way the programs have controlled total costs in the state is to hold down increases for specific categories, such as doctor fees and hospital costs. Some states have switched to a DRG-based payment system for Medicaid, with mixed success in controlling costs. Others have clamped down on inflation in hospital fees. In fact, Medicaid shortfalls are the fastest-growing component of unreimbursed hospital care for the poor. This gap leads to cost shifting to other payment sources, especially patients with private insurance through work. Thus the impact of Medicaid shortfalls reverberates throughout the entire health care system.

Overall Cost Containment

Clearly, overall cost containment has been one of the major issues facing health policymakers for the past 20 years. Compared to other countries and other time periods, health care expenses have been increasing greatly in the past 20 years. Why is the United States unable to contain health care costs successfully? One simple but accurate answer is that we have an open system with numerous sources of funds (Ginzberg, 1987). This country does not have controls on the amount of resources going into health care, unlike most other countries in the world (Rice, 1992). No one entity controls costs, in comparison to Great Britain or Canada, where politicians play a role in determining funding levels for health care as for all other types of programs. All of these controls do not necessarily occur at the national level. In Canada, provincial controls also operate. There is clear evidence that the most effective cost containment strategies are those aimed at providers in situations with one payor for care—the government. Whether such reforms are likely will be one part of the topics addressed in Chapter 9. Many experts would agree that without such reforms, efforts at cost containment will not be very successful (Ginzberg, 1987; Glaser, 1986; Rice, 1992).

8

Quality of Health Care Technology

Quality is the third leg of the three-legged stool of essential elements in health services research and health care delivery, with the other two being costs and access. No evaluation of a health care system or discussion of health care policy issues is complete without attention to quality. Once we talk about quality, we are also talking about evaluation and measurement of health systems outputs, since defining and examining quality is necessarily an evaluative process. One difficulty in the area of quality, as compared to the that of cost, is that measurement is less clear and the health care system in the United States is not easily amenable to evaluation. No clear and complete consensus exists about how to measure health care system outputs or quality. Partially this is due to a lack of clear definition, as already discussed, about what health actually is. Also, the linkages between the health care system and the production of health, even if we simplistically define health as the reduction in the amount of death, is not always clear, as recent research has demonstrated (McKeown, 1979; McKinlay & McKinlay, 1977).

Quality is often defined as the degree of excellence or confirmation to standards. It cannot be assessed without a clear understanding about the expected standards of excellence. One difficulty is that society's expectations of health and medical care are not clearly delineated; moreover, the quality of care is inextricably intertwined with societal, professional, and patient expectations concerning the role of health care in the society.

In the absence of this clarity, this chapter will focus first on various approaches to defining quality, then on a review of quality control efforts in health, those emanating from both the federal government and private groups. This will include the approaches to quality assessment that were started over the past 30 years, as well as the newer emphases on linking quality of care to redefinition of clinical standards. Last, the chapter will raise some questions about the future of quality control and assessment efforts in health care and will discuss the importance of paying attention to quality, however difficult it is to measure and define, if more comprehensive health care system reforms are implemented by the end of this century.

Basic Components of Quality Assessment: Structure, Process, and Outcome

One classic approach to the assessment of quality in health care, especially as related to patient care, is to divide aspects of quality into three components; structure, process, and outcome (Brook, Williams, & Davis-Avery, 1976; Donabedian, 1968; Donabedian, Wheeler, & Wyszewianski, 1982). The simplest in terms of availability of information is structure. Measures of structure of care relate to both personnel and facilities used to provide services and the manner in which they are organized. Much of this information can be readily obtained from existing documents. An example of structural measures for facilities would be whether the facility meets fire and safety codes. An example of a structural measure for quality of physician care would be whether physicians are licensed and board certified. The general opinion is that while such measures are important (and often form the basis for state requirements for licensure, certification, and accreditation), they are not sufficient to guarantee that the actual process of care is good or that outcomes are optimal.

Licensure as a type of structural measure of quality is the most pervasive, the most basic, and the oldest quality assurance approach. Licensure is used for most health care professions. While traditionally it has been a very static approach, and a person's right to practice was rarely challenged once he or she was licensed, a number of states are now requiring continuing education as a way of assuring that knowledge remains up to date. Disciplinary actions by licensure boards are another way to ensure quality in problematic cases, and in the past 10 years there has been somewhat greater usage of revocation or restriction of licensure, particularly as connected with serious alcohol or drug use. In the United States, licensure of professionals is typically a state function. Certification by specialty boards is another common type of assurance of structural quality. The groups that perform this review are private, not public. Licensure of facilities is also a state function, but these certifications have often focused narrowly on structure. A whole separate commission has been created to examine quality in the institutional setting. These standards have become increasingly national due to the impact of the Medicare and Medicaid programs, which require that care be delivered in accredited institutions. This has particularly impacted on non-hospital facilities, such as nursing homes, because most hospitals have participated in quality reviews since the process was started in 1951. This process of institutional accreditation will be discussed in more detail in the next section of this chapter.

Process measures typically reflect what was actually done to a patient, such as the numbers and types of procedures and laboratory tests that were performed (Donabedian, 1968). This has also often been defined as the content of care (DeGeyndt, 1970). A frequent extension is to separate technical aspects of care from the affective and interpersonal aspects of care (Brook et al., 1976). One advantage of this approach over moving to outcome measures is that process of care, at least the technical aspect, is usually well documented in the medical record. One major caveat of process measures is that the linkage between the process, what is done to a patient, and the outcome is not always clear.

Outcome measures reflect the outcomes or impacts of care. Another way to think of outcome measures are as net changes that occur in health status as a result of the medical care received. Many experts now favor greater emphasis on outcomes to assess quality. This approach is not without controversy, however. One major concern is that many factors affect health, not just the care received, and too simplistic a focus on outcomes does not reflect these various factors. Another concern is that for outcomes to be used as an indicator of quality of care, the outcomes need to be sensitive to different levels in the process or content of care, and not all outcomes are.

Two different examples help to illustrate the difficulties in moving to outcomes as the major indicator of quality. One example relates to long-term care facilities. What would be an appropriate outcome-oriented measure of care in such a facility? Given that most patients enter these facilities because recovery is not expected, and the majority live there until their death, outcomes that focus on whether the patient recovers would declare all such facilities failures. Obviously, different intermediate level outcomes are needed, such as whether bedridden patients develop bedsores and whether patients without mental complications remain as active as possible and mentally alert.

The other example of problems stemming from the simplistic use of outcome data as a measure of quality relates to the release of hospital mortality data, which the Health Care Financing Administration (HCFA) has made available to the public for the past few years. This information is now routinely publicized by the media, and hospitals with high mortality rates in specific areas often are upset over this new approach. Even a quick review of these lists of high mortality hospitals indicates that some of the best-known hospitals in the United States, connected with major medical schools, have appeared on the list. Yet no one really believes they have among the worst quality of care in the country. Those hospitals have high mortality rates because they are tertiary care facilities and have patients referred to them who are already in very poor health and nonresponsive to traditional therapies. Thus a more accurate comparison would need to adjust for such factors as patient's beginning health status. These two examples illustrate how it is far easier to talk about using outcome as a measure of quality of care than it would be to implement such an approach.

Joint Commission Activities

What are the major kinds of approaches used to measure quality of care currently? The major institutional-based approach is conducted by the Joint Commission on Accreditation of Health Care Organizations (JCAHO), formerly known as the Joint Commission on the Accreditation of Hospitals (JCAH). Other approaches relate to federally mandated programs and will be discussed in the following section. The JCAHO is the most important nongovernmental quality control effort in health care. This group functions as an influential accreditation body and has expanded its role, since its founding in 1951, from accreditation of hospitals to accreditation of nursing homes, many outpatient facilities, mental and behavioral health and psychiatric services, and hospice services, as well as more general traditional short-term stay hospitals.

JCAHO functions as an independent accrediting body, with representation from the American Hospital Association, the American Medical Association, the American College of Surgery, the American College of Physicians, and the American Dental Association. Accreditation by JCAHO is a voluntary process, but almost three-quarters of all hospitals in the United States seek its accreditation. Of those with 200 or more beds, more than 95% are accredited (Logerfo & Brook, 1988).

Historically, JCAHO began with a structural approach to quality and maintained standards for safety, medical records, control of hospital infection, and tissue review for surgery. The approach has been changing to a greater emphasis on process- and performance-based assessment of quality, with documentation of deficiencies that were found and how they were corrected. Also, initially the standards applied to the medical staff and delegated quality assurance concerns to them. Today, JCAHO standards place the responsibility with the trustees, in concert with the medical staff. Currently, the JCAHO is moving toward an emphasis on outcomes and documentation of outcomes of care, in addition to structural features and process measures. One current controversy about this shift is the concern about how to document outcomes. Many hospitals complain that they will have to allocate more resources to data collection efforts for the JCAHO accreditation. In addition, problems of what outcomes should be examined remain.

Initial Federal Quality Control Efforts

The implementation of the Medicare and Medicaid programs began a role for the federal government in setting quality standards. Much of this role in the early days was delegated to states via the state role in certification of facilities and licensure of physicians, since the major requirement was that practitioners be licensed and facilities certified in their own states. By 1972 a new quality control effort was set up by the federal government, the Professional Standards Review Organizations (PSROs). These organizations were composed of committees of practicing physicians who were to provide effective oversight of medical services paid for through the Medicare and Medicaid programs. These organizations mostly reviewed records and made recommendations, having limited options for either punishment or changing behavior.

Because of the lack of "teeth" in the PSRO legislation, new laws passed in 1982 created PROs (Peer Review Organizations). These are contracted groups of physicians, typically on a statewide basis, that are charged with reviewing the professional activities of physicians, other practitioners, and institutional providers of service to Medicare beneficiaries. The PRO program is administered by the Health Care Financing Administration (HCFA), the agency responsible for Medicare and Medicaid. HCFA has charged the PROs with "applying professionally developed criteria of care, diagnosis and treatment based on typical practice patterns within your geographic area or national criteria, where appropriate, to evaluate the medical necessity, quality or appropriateness of the items or services ordered or furnished by providers and practitioners." The 1991 budget for the program was $330 million, making it a sizable effort financially (Kellie & Kelly, 1991).

The amount of work required by PROs has been increasing. In the first scope of work, from 1984 to 1986, the PROs were to carry out preprocedure reviews for five procedures. Under the scope of work from 1988 to 1990, PROs had to conduct such reviews for 10 major conditions and part of 11 others. A recent review of the effectiveness of this process in the third period concluded that there was significant variability in the application of the same explicit criteria from PRO to PRO (Kellie & Kelly, 1991). For this and other reasons, the PRO process has been controversial, and physicians in some states have at times become so unhappy that they have pushed for the replacement of one PRO with another, as occurred in Arkansas in 1989 (Golden, 1990). One conclusion of a recent study and several recent reports from the Institute of Medicine about the quality assessment process was that criteria need to be made public so that studies of variability can occur (Institute of Medicine, 1989, 1990; Kellie & Kelly, 1991). The same reports also conclude that there needs to be greater attention paid to content and methods used to develop review criteria.

Newer Quality Issues

Quality, both in health care and in many other areas in society, has been receiving more attention recently. Within health care, two major efforts have impacted both upon definitions of quality and upon policy debates about the role of the federal government. In addition, a third approach, from general business, is one of the major new controversies within general management. A recent business trend taken from Japanese management is an emphasis on total quality. This is a very new concept to be applied within health care and will be discussed first. Within health care, one effort has been the development of research to try to better understand patient outcomes and how they link to health care practice. This federally financed and directed effort will be discussed second. The third major effort has already been mentioned, the review of the Institute of Medicine about the role of PROs and quality assessment within health care more generally. The implications of that review and critique will also be reviewed.

Total Quality Management or TQM

One major trend has been the growth of new approaches to quality in the industrial sector, often known as TQM or total quality management. While this approach is derived from industrial engineering and operations research approaches within business, there is increased interest in applying it within health care. The TQM concept, and its growing acceptance within general business circles, has raised questions about quality within health care to a broader audience, especially human resources managers in business who are responsible for the selection of health insurance options for employees. TQM assumes that the strategic orientation of the organization is managed on a daily basis with an emphasis on quality. Part of the notion includes a shared vision within the organization, and important within health care would be a shared vision between physicians and other health care workers in a hospital. The concept is just beginning to be applied in the health care area. In more general businesses, the concept has often included an emphasis on the consumer and attention to consumer concerns about a product. If applied to health care, the concept could focus greater attention on the rights of patients as consumers and the importance of patient opinions and evaluations.

This is a controversial issue, since one traditional underpinning of quality assessment in health care has been the need for peer evaluation, and the corresponding inability of patients to actually evaluate technical quality. While most health care experts would continue to argue that patients who are not technically trained cannot evaluate the details of care, a focus on TQM approaches within health care may bring the rights and attitudes of patients to a more prominent role within the health care system. An additional controversy that this approach may imply is an emphasis on the total team providing care, and thus the relative role of physicians may be deemphasized.

The PORTs Effort and Related Background

Research on the quality of health care was initially supported in the federal government by the National Center for Health Services Research. In the late 1960s this agency funded a research and demonstration program, EMCRO (Experimental Medical Care Review Organizations), that focused on the development of process measures of care and became the basis for the development of PSROs (Salive, Mayfield, & Weissman, 1990). In 1986 Congress established the Patient Outcome Assessment research program with funding from the Medicare Trust Fund (Bowen & Burke, 1988; Salive et al., 1990). This program mandated a greater emphasis on quality examination within Medicare and Medicaid and charged HCFA, along with NCHSR, with the responsibility to develop a medical treatment effectiveness initiative. Initial studies were funded to examine treatment for heart disease, hypertension, diabetes, rheumatoid arthritis, coronary artery bypass surgery, and several other specialized problems.

By 1990 NCHSR was transformed into a new agency, the Agency for Health Care Policy and Research (AHCPR) and, along with HCFA, jointly charged with the responsibility for creating MEDTEP, the Medical Treatment and Effectiveness Program. Congressional authorizations provide for funding as high as $185 million by 1994. The MEDTEP program has four elements: medical treatment effectiveness research, development of databases for such research, development of clinical guidelines, and the dissemination of research findings and clinical guidelines. The specific name for the effectiveness research program is PORTs (Patient Outcomes Research Teams). PORT projects include a review and formal synthesis of available research to serve as the basis for specifying research hypotheses. Then the PORTs are to collect and analyze data to identify and explain variations in clinical practice and patient outcomes. PORTs have been funded to study acute myocardial infarction, locally invasive prostatic carcinoma, low back pain, cataracts, colon cancer, hip fracture, chronic ischemic heart disease, stroke, and several smaller more specialized problems. The goal of PORTs is to produce a leaner, trimmer health care system, in which procedures that are effective can be funded and spread through the country, and procedures that are not can be eliminated. How well is this approach working? Since most PORTs were funded for 5 years and funding generally did not begin until 1990, it is too early for a complete assessment. Several concerns and controversies have arisen about this process. Some researchers argue that too many funds are being concentrated on these few projects and that utility may be limited. Some practicing physicians fear that researchers removed from the reality of patients and the clinical situation will make decisions to eliminate procedures that are helpful to individual patients.

Preliminary results from the low back pain and myocardial infarction studies are already generating controversy (AHCPR, 1991). Initial work from the lower back pain PORT indicates that most episodes of low back pain improve rapidly with little or no intervention and that few patients even require plain X-rays, much less more sophisticated treatment (AHCPR, 1991). The PORT examining myocardial infarction has so far examined 1986 HCFA data to find that there is threefold variation in the use of cardiac catheterization procedures among states, with the lowest rate in the Northeast and the highest in the Southeast and Plains states. More work remains to be done on the implications of the variation, but this research has the potential to ultimately recommend large reductions in the performance of this common and financially lucrative procedure.

The Institute of Medicine Critique, MOS Studies, and Suggestions for Change

The Institute of Medicine recently released the results of a study on quality assurance for the Medicare Program (Institute of Medicine, 1989, 1990). The overall conclusions of these reports was that while quality of care in Medicare was not bad, it could be improved, and that the current system to assess quality of care is not very effective (Lohr & Schroeder, 1990). They found overuse of some care, underuse of others, and poor technical and interpersonal performance in some cases. A review of 5,000 records indicated overuse, in that 17% of coronary angiographies were probably not needed. Antibiotics were widely misused, with one community study reporting that 28% of therapeutic uses and 64% of preventive or prophylactic uses were inappropriate (Jogerst & Dippe, 1981). Underuse is harder to find, but there appeared to be evidence that common problems in the elderly, such as incontinence, gait disorders, and depression, were often not treated, perhaps because they were viewed as "typical" consequences of aging.

Critiques of the role of PROs are important for any long-term change in quality assessment. Many of the errors identified and issues of questionable treatment cannot be thoroughly addressed until some of the PORT studies are concluded. One recent series of studies already released are the MOS or Medical Outcomes Studies, which examined differences in the mix of patients among medical specialists and organizational systems of care (Kravitz, Greenfield, Rogers, Manning, Zubkoff, Nelson, Tarlov, & Ware, 1992; Rosenblatt, 1992). While this study did find that older and sicker patients gravitate to more specialized physicians, it also found that even after controlling for patient mix, sub-specialists such as endocrinologists and cardiologists used more resources to treat patients than general internists and family practitioners. Still incomplete is the portion of the study that will address whether these variations in intensity of resource use affect biological outcomes. These will be critical results to obtain.

Some changes in the quality assessment systems of PROs could occur even while we wait for better studies and further results. Many problems with PROs could change. The IOM report concluded that PROs still focus too much of their efforts on control of utilization and cost issues, rather than on actual quality issues. In addition, this focus on over-utilization and cost has been interpreted by many providers to be adversarial and punitive, and thus little new learning of better treatment approaches occurs through the process. Too many of the reviews focus on individual events, rather than on total episodes of care or average practice. In addition, almost all reviews focus on inpatient care, yet outpatient care is increasing more rapidly and may currently reflect even more variable quality standards.

Finally, despite the possibility of sanctions, the actual application of sanctions is limited. Fewer than 100 sanctions have been forwarded by HCFA to the Office of the Inspector General in recent years (Lohr & Schroeder, 1990). Recommendations are that revised PRO efforts give more attention to patient-practitioner interaction, broad health and quality-of-life indicators, and patient satisfaction and well-being. These ideas would tie in with a revised approach to quality assessment in line with such business changes as the TQM approach. As part of this, one recommendation is to move PROs away from a focus on utilization or cost control to a clearer focus on quality, possibly through the implementation of a new Medicare Program to Assure Quality or MPAQ. Such a new approach would require more money. Many experts believe reform of the quality control system should be part of a comprehensive health care system reform. Most experts expect continued attention to quality throughout the 1990s.

Malpractice and Quality Linkages

One of the debates in the U.S. health care system the past 10 years has been over rising rates of malpractice insurance. Many physicians have argued that rates have gone up so much because of frivolous suits and the propensity of Americans to turn to the courts for remedies. Physicians have argued that insurance companies settle out of court and give large awards, even where no negligence has occurred, just to avoid the costs of a jury trial and the inherent instability of large awards from a jury. One critical linkage with quality is whether there is more actual malpractice occurring today (since it is clear that the rate of filings and suits is up in many states). There is some evidence that a decline in strong doctor-patient relationships and the greater anonymity of large cities and practices might be important factors in the rate of malpractice suits filed. One policy controversy in the malpractice area has been whether it would be better to eliminate legal suits and have an arbitration system.

What do malpractice data tell us about the rate of medical error, which is in many ways the reverse side of quality, and the importance of suits? A review of data from California found little evidence that hospital or physician errors occurred less frequently recently than in 1974 (Feldman & Roblin, 1992; Mills, 1977). In a very comprehensive analysis of hospital medical records from New York State, the incidence of adverse events was 3.7%. More than one-quarter (27.6 %) were considered to be negligent. Fourteen percent of adversely affected patients died, at least in part due to the adverse event (Harvard Medical Practice Study, 1990). The risk of sustaining an adverse event increased with age, and the percent resulting from negligence was increased in elderly patients, arguing for the importance of increased PRO activity for Medicare patients. Although half of all adverse events occurred in patients undergoing surgery, the percent caused by negligence in surgery was lower, demonstrating that surgical procedures will always carry some inherent risk. Evidence on the deterrent effect of actual suits from the Harvard study was mixed, leading to no clear policy recommendations.

What are the remaining controversies in quality? One important conclusion from the Harvard study is the need to continue to review records and try to improve quality and reduce the rates of adverse effects. Another conclusion may be that there will always be some adverse effects. Thus, it is not possible to have all procedures always be risk-free. In providing health care services to individuals, there will always be some chance of a problem developing. This increases the importance of knowing the general efficacy of procedures and treatment, so that only useful treatments and procedures occur. Unnecessary risk clearly produces lowered quality of care. Thus research on patient outcomes is essential to continue quality improvement in health care.

9

Access to Health Care Services and
Suggestions for Health Care Reform

The issue of access to health care services and the related issues concerning health care reform are becoming the major issues in health care today. Obviously, the issues of access to care, provision of uncompensated care, and system reform are not new issues for the health care system to confront. At the beginning of this book, we discussed the overused term *health care crisis.* One important factor people consider in describing a current crisis in the U.S. health care system is the issue of access to care.

Over the years, there have been many debates about what the basic rights are that a society owes to any citizen. While different people would come up with different essential elements, there is no denying that one factor that distinguishes the United States from all other industrialized countries (with the exception of South Africa) is the lack of clarity as to whether the United States regards health care access as a basic human right (Davis, Gold, & Maleac, 1981; Kronenfeld & Whicker, 1984; Mullan, 1987). In almost all other countries, a citizen who becomes ill has a right to receive health care, often fairly comprehensive health care. Not all other countries achieve this goal with the same type of health care system. Some have a true national health care system, which, in following a more socialistic model, covers the person's health care needs from cradle to grave. Others have a much more complex system, which employs different health insurance mechanisms. What is true, however, is that in these other countries people who are ill or worried about their health have a mechanism to receive at least initial health care. Depending upon the problem, the person may then have to wait for a particular service, or might even not be told about the newest technology that might be available to wealthy, well-insured individuals in the United States. Almost all experts agree, however, that coverage for basic care is complete and simpler to obtain in most other countries than it is in the United States.

Equity and a Right to Care

Two major issues relating to coverage for health care and access to care in the United States are concepts of equity and of whether health care is viewed as a basic right. Equity as a concept is a complex issue. What does equity mean? Does equity imply equal access to health care for all groups, or equal health care, not just access? This debate is not unique to health care. One of the current issues in education is whether the goal is to spend the same amount of money on all students; to allow great variation from area to area, with an emphasis on local control of schools; or to ensure that all students have similar achievements (or outcomes, as are discussed in the health care area). A more basic way to address this issue of equity is to consider whether the goal of a just society is equal opportunity to achieve or acquire—or equal results. One complication in health care is that there are large degrees of physiological and genetic variability in initial levels of health and serious health problems. Moreover, access to the basic goods of society, such as adequate food, housing and clothing, at a young age can influence a person's health status. Thus, from data in earlier chapters, we know that the poor are less healthy than those who are not poor. Does equity require greater health care access by the less healthy, or at least greater consumption of health care resources, since the need in those groups is higher?

There are two coexistent but contradictory traditions in the United States about access to services, especially health care services (Kronenfeld & Whicker, 1984). One tradition contends that individuals are responsible for their own welfare, including health care. The other holds that communities do have a responsibility for providing health care access to all citizens, especially those unable to secure access on their own.

Prior Attempts to Pass National Health Insurance and Ensure Access to Care

The Committee on the Cost of Medical Care in 1932 was one of the earliest systematic attempts in the United States to study the economics of health care and access issues. Supported by private foundations, this committee negated a then-popular conception that good medical care was widely available to the poor as well as the rich. This committee reported persistent gaps for different geographic units, rural and urban regions, and income groups (Falk, 1983).

There were moves at that time (early 1930s), with the creation of the Social Security System of the New Deal under President Franklin Roosevelt, to add health coverage for the elderly to the system. The initial program that was suggested bore a strong resemblance to what was eventually passed as the Medicare program in 1965. Due to the AMA's opposition to including health care in the Social Security Bill, and the fear that organized opposition from such a strong group might lead to the defeat of the entire bill, the health-related portions were deleted.

This issue did not come up again until after World War II. Then, despite moves to enact some form of national health insurance under President Truman, the Hill-Burton Act, to subsidize building of hospitals and begin some state-based health planning, was passed instead. One of the earliest national commissions to deal with access to health care and equity issues was commissioned by President Eisenhower and concluded that "access to the means for attainment and preservation of health is a basic human right" (President's Commission on the Health Needs of the Nation, 1953). This philosophy became important in guiding federal health policy efforts to increase access to health care, but within a model of the existing health care system.

By the early 1960s concern had grown over two groups with special access problems, the elderly and the poor. In 1960 the Kerr-Mills Act was passed to begin, on a limited scale, the provision of direct medical assistance and payment for health care services for the elderly poor. This legislation was greatly expanded and superseded by the passage of

Medicare, providing basic health care insurance for the elderly, and Medicaid, a joint federal/state program providing health care services to some of the poor, particularly those receiving joint federal/state welfare payments.

Since then, there have been several periods when there was major agitation about health care system reform and discussion of implementing some form of national health insurance. There have two instances in the past 25 years when many health care experts felt we were close to enacting more major reforms. One was during the second term of President Nixon, in the period before the Watergate episode became public knowledge. Rising health care costs were one important factor behind the push for reform at that time, as were disclosures about both problems in access and the limitations of the Medicare-Medicaid programs. The Democratic proposals in Congress and the Republican proposals backed by Nixon were moving closer to a system of mandatory national health insurance. As the Watergate crisis became public knowledge and then deepened, all other issues received less attention in Congress, and the momentum disappeared.

The second period was during the presidential campaign of 1976, when Jimmy Carter, a Democrat, was elected. Health care reform had been an important issue pushed by major Democrats in Congress. National health insurance became a major plank in the platform adopted at the nominating convention that year. Experts believed that Carter would push vigorously for such a program, and given the Democrats' control of Congress, that such reforms would be enacted. Instead, inflation rates zoomed, and Carter never really pushed on such legislation. Again, the momentum for reform was lost. Once Carter lost the campaign for reelection in 1980 to Ronald Reagan, comprehensive health care reform moved off the health care agenda, although cost control and quality measures, such as discussed in the preceding chapters, were implemented.

During this time, another presidential commission was appointed to review issues of equity and ethics in health care. In a report released in 1983 while Reagan was president, this commission concluded that society has an ethical obligation to ensure equitable access to health care for all (President's Commission for the Study of Ethical Problems, 1983). Reasons cited in the commission report were the special importance of health care in the quality of life, and recognition that health care needs are generally beyond individual control. Balancing the societal obligation were individual obligations to pay a "fair share" of their own health care costs and to take reasonable steps to provide for such care.

The commission again questioned what equity in health care is and defined it as access to a standard level of care without incurring excessive burdens. This was translated into a policy recommendation of a minimum level of adequate care below which no one should fall. Reflecting the more conservative tenor of the Reagan administration, the commission explicitly did not exclude differences in health care access and did not set any ceiling on total amounts of care for an individual. It also endorsed the desirability of achieving equity through private market forces whenever possible. On balance, however, the report did conclude that the final responsibility for health care rests with the federal government, working through a combination of government and private forces.

Current Differentials in Access
to Care and Health Insurance

While limited access to health care due to lack of health insurance was a problem even during the initiation and expansion of Great Society programs and Medicaid, there is general agreement that the problem is larger today than in the 1970s. Who are those with limited access to care and who end up in hospitals, unable to pay for their care (often called the uncompensated care group in discussions of hospital care)? Typically, the uncompensated care population consists of people with one or some combination of the following problems: poor health, poverty, and the absence of health insurance. Often, the presence of one of these alone may bring minor problems in access, while a person with a combination of two or all three often has unpaid bills of thousands of dollars, or may even be a person whose health is ruined by delayed receipt of health care. The uncompensated care population includes many young people; perhaps one-third are children. More than half of those lacking health insurance are employed for at least part of the year (Cohodes, 1986). The term *uncompensated care* lacks a clear meaning. In some way, the care is compensated or paid for, but not by the recipient of care. Often, hospitals talk of two components of uncompensated care: bad debt (costs accrued by individuals who should be able to pay but fail to do so) and charity care (care given to people who not only do not and cannot pay, but were never expected to pay).

Most uncompensated care is provided in hospitals. In 1984 the American Hospital Association estimated that $5.7 billion of uncompensated care (measured in costs, not charges) was provided. This comprised 4.6% of hospital costs, up from 3.6% in 1980. Not all hospitals share this burden equally; more is borne by public, general, and teaching hospitals. It has been estimated that for public hospitals, about 11.5% of all costs in 1983 were for uncompensated care (Sherlock, 1986).

While there is a range of estimates about the numbers of people uninsured and underinsured in the United States from the early 1980s on, most sources agree that there has been an increase in the numbers of uninsured since the late 1970s (Freeman, Blendon, Aiken, Sudman, Mullinix, & Corey, 1987; Kasper, 1987; Robert Wood Johnson Foundation, 1987; Wilensky & Ladenheim, 1987). What are the trends in limited access, uninsured, and underinsured, and the related trends in utilization of health care services? The United States has always had many uninsured individuals. Traditionally, especially prior to the Medicaid program, income was a major determinant of access to care, especially access to outpatient and physician services. Several studies have demonstrated that the gap in levels of physician use between the poor and the rest of society has narrowed over the past 20 years (Aday, Anderson, & Fleming, 1980; Wilson & White, 1977). In many aspects of utilization today, the poor as a group actually use a higher number of services than do the nonpoor. On the average, the poor are less healthy than the nonpoor. This is true for many measures of acute illness and is particularly true for chronic illness. Thus it is appropriate for the poor, given their higher level of illness and resulting greater need for care, to utilize more health care services than the nonpoor. Disagreement has remained about the extent to which the poor may underutilize care, relative to their need for care (Kleinman et al., 1981).

In the late 1970s the best estimates were that 25 to 26 million people in the United States were without health care insurance. This was about 13% of the population under 65. The numbers of uninsured grew in the 1980s. Estimates in 1992 range from a low of 22 million to a high of 37 million. The source that estimated the figure as low as 22 million agreed that there had been a decrease in access between 1982 and 1986, the two dates of its studies, but simply arrived at lower figures in the earlier years and in the later years than did other sources (Robert Wood Johnson Foundation, 1987). The Census Bureau has the highest estimate, 37 million, while the most accurate estimate is probably around 31 million

(Moyer, 1989; U.S. Bureau of the Census, 1986b; Wilensky, 1987; Wilensky & Ladenheim, 1987).

Who are the estimated 30 million or more Americans who have neither private health insurance nor coverage for health care services under public insurance programs such as Medicare and Medicaid? They are not a homogeneous group. While some are those we might assume are the major groups with the problem—the homeless, the socially dislocated—others are people who either work part or all of the year, but have no health insurance coverage, or are temporarily unemployed. Surprising to some people, those without insurance even include some relatively high-income families in which the primary breadwinner has a serious chronic illness, can no longer work, and yet is not a recipient of public health insurance programs.

In 1987 almost half of the uninsured were children or were in families with children (Moyer, 1989). In addition, more than half of the uninsured were concentrated in the South and West census regions (Moyer, 1989). Fewer than one-third of the uninsured were poor, and an additional 9% were near poor (in families with incomes below 125% of the poverty threshold). The largest group of uninsured individuals was in families with incomes above 185% of the poverty level (Moyer, 1989).

Critical to understanding how some groups of people have no health insurance in American society is the realization that most private health insurance in the United States is purchased through employer-based group insurance policies. This represents about 85% of all private coverage. One major factor in the increase in the number of uninsured in the 1980s was the growth in unemployment in the early 1980s and again in the early 1990s. It is less clear why the rate of uninsured did not return to previously lower levels following the economic recovery in the mid-1980s and improvement in the unemployment rate. Possible explanations are shifts in type of employment (such as from manufacturing jobs to service jobs), shifts in the number of part-time versus full-time jobs, and Medicaid's failure to keep up with rising poverty levels.

Shifts in the sector of employment and shifts in the number of part-time versus full-time jobs are both related to ongoing changes in the economy. Many experts believe the United States is moving from a manufacturing-dominated economy to a service economy. Typical changes would be a decrease in the number of people employed in automobile manufacturing (a group with extensive health insurance coverage) and an increase in the number of people employed in fast food establishments. Many of these latter jobs pay only the minimum wage and often employ a large group of part-time workers. Typically, these part-time workers do not receive such benefits as health insurance. If the part-time worker is a high school student covered under parents' insurance, or a person over 65 supplementing Social Security income, the lack of health insurance provision in these jobs does not lead to an increase in the number of uninsured Americans. If these jobs are filled by heads of households or single adults who cannot obtain other jobs, there is an impact on the number of persons without health insurance.

Almost 17 million of the uninsured were employed more than 18 hours a week for all or part of 1987. Of these uninsured employed people, more than half worked full-time all of 1987. About 43%, however, worked for firms with fewer than 25 employees. In one 1988 survey, 49% of uninsured workers were self-employed or were in firms of fewer than 25 workers (Health Insurance Association of America, 1990). Almost 80% of the uninsured were employed or dependents of employed persons in 1987 (Moyer, 1989). This includes workers in low-wage industries and workers in agriculture, forestry, construction, personal services, and retail trade. Agriculture is the industry with the current lowest coverage: 16% uninsured throughout the year (Wilensky & Ladenheim, 1987). Individuals in low-paid jobs are less likely to be insured. In 1985, almost 70% of workers without coverage earned less than $10,000. Most of the rest earned less than $20,000.

The poor and near poor are another major group without health insurance, with more than 40% of the uninsured falling into these categories (some of these people are also part of the working uninsured). Why are these people not covered by Medicaid, the jointly funded federal/state program to provide health care services to the poor? Welfare coverage has not kept up with rising inflation over the past two decades and there are limitations of welfare programs based, as in most states, on specific categories of eligible people. In 1976 Medicaid covered 65% of poor Americans, but this had shrunk as low as 38% by 1983 (Mowll, 1989). As high rates of inflation hit in the latter half of the 1970s, most states did not raise their welfare eligibility levels to keep up with rising incomes and rising costs of basics such as housing, food, and utilities. In addition, many states provided limited or no Medicaid coverage for two-person working poor families, families in which the worker was more likely to be employed in the sectors least likely to offer health insurance.

There is another group of people with no insurance—those with a history of serious medical problems. Many people with serious health problems do maintain health insurance coverage as long as they keep their jobs. If they lose their current jobs, due to the general economy or their health, but can still work, they may experience problems in finding employment because of their health. Not only do businesses not want employees with illnesses that may require repeated absences, but increasingly health insurance companies are "experience-rating" individual company policies. A workplace with a few high utilizers of health care due to chronic illness can raise the insurance rates for the entire company. Employers are thus reluctant to hire a worker who may increase overall costs in this area. While people who are medically uninsurable are a small part of those without health insurance, they represent a much larger proportion of the uncompensated care expenses because they are very high utilizers of health services. Recent studies have estimated that .5% to 1% of the U.S. population is currently "medically uninsurable" (Wilensky & Ladenheim, 1987). A growing concern is that the spread of AIDS is increasing these numbers.

One last way to examine who has problems obtaining health care is to look at data from health interview surveys concerning visits to health care providers and actual health status. The Robert Wood Johnson Foundation sponsored national access surveys in 1976, 1982, and 1986 (Robert Wood Johnson Foundation, 1978, 1983, 1987). Problems with access remain among some groups. Eighteen percent of all respondents reported no regular source of care in the past year. The percentage of persons with no ambulatory care visits also increased, from about 20% in 1982 to 33% in 1986. This led to a decline in the average number of visits, from 4.8 to 4.3 per year. Most important as an indicator of access problems, the gap in use of health care and access to health insurance between poor and nonpoor who are in fair or poor health increased. The nonpoor in fair or poor health had 37% more ambulatory care visits than did the poor with the same health status. While only 4% of the nonpoor with chronic illness lack health insurance, about 12% of the poor with a chronic or serious illness have no health insurance. Special groups in the population also reported more serious access problems in 1986. Among Hispanics, for example, the percentage reporting no regular source of care tripled, up to 30% (Robert Wood Johnson Foundation, 1987). Recent work with other data sets has also demonstrated the importance of barriers in access to health care among Hispanics (Wolinsky, Aguirre, & Fans, 1989).

The proportion of uninsured continues to creep up. Recent preliminary data from studies by the Employee Benefits Research Institute found that proportion increasing between its 1988 and 1990 surveys. The institute's data has indicated an uninsured rate of 15.9% in 1988, and 16.6% in 1990. The percentages are particularly high for families earning lower incomes, with the proportion of non-elderly population without health insurance almost 30% in 1990, both for families earning less than $10,000 and for families earning $10,000 to $20,000 a year (Somerville, 1992).

What about the link between health outcomes and access to care? There have been a number of recent studies exploring specific services and the linkages between health outcomes and access to care (Baquet & Ringen, 1987; Davis, 1991; Hadley, Steinberg, & Feder, 1991; Lurie, Ward, Shapiro, & Brook, 1984). In a study examining the impact on health status of being dropped from coverage by MediCal (California's version of Medicaid) in the early 1980s, the number of people with untreated diabetes and hypertension increased (Lurie et al., 1984). The probability of death was greater for those losing MediCal coverage than for a control group retaining coverage. A different study found that incidence and mortality of cervical cancer is two to three times higher in blacks than in whites and attributed these findings to differentials in access to care (Baquet & Ringen, 1987). Even when the uninsured make it to a hospital, their outcomes differ. The uninsured who were hospitalized in one study were less likely to get specialized services and more likely to die (Hadley et al., 1991). Actual in-hospital death rates were 1.2 to 3.4 times as high among uninsured patients as among privately insured patients, after taking account statistically of the poorer health status of the uninsured upon admission to the hospital.

Lessons to Be Learned: State Reforms, Past Efforts, and International Comparisons

State Reforms

In the United States, especially in the areas of health and social services, reforms often are initiated at state levels. One trend in a number of states in the 1980s was the mandating of benefits, or states requiring health insurance for everyone. An early innovator, which required that health insurance to be provided by all employers, is the state of Hawaii, which passed such legislation in 1974. This has increased coverage in the state and appears to be working well there. The plan requires all businesses to provide health insurance for those working at least 20 hours a week (Burke, 1992). Current estimates are that 87% of Hawaii's residents are insured, another 7% are covered by Medicaid, and the SHIP (State Health Insurance Program) provides a minimum level of coverage to almost all others. This minimum level of coverage includes immunizations, wellness checkups and other preventive care, 12 physician visits a year, and 5 hospital days (including 2 for maternity care). The uniqueness of Hawaii's recent plantation past and the provision of health care services by plantation owners, as well as the geographical isolation of the state, which makes it difficult for employers to decide to leave and move to another state, have led some experts to argue that it is difficult to generalize to other states from the Hawaii experience. In any case, few states followed this innovation quickly (in the next 10 years).

Mandating benefits (such as that pregnancy, infertility, mental health, or drug abuse benefits must be provided if any health insurance is provided) has been one approach a number of states implemented in the 1980s to reduce both the number of people without health insurance and the range of conditions not covered. An advantage of mandates to the public (and often to the lawmakers) is that they do not require a tax increase. One common type of mandated benefit covers specific services. Alcoholism is required to be covered to some extent by 37 states, mental health coverage by 28, and maternity services by 18. Another type of mandate is that services of certain providers be covered, especially chiropractors and psychologists (36 states) and optometrists (30). The third type of mandate dictates that certain categories of people be included such as newborns (38 states) and adopted children (18 states).

How useful has the mandate approach been, how much does it cost, and who bears the cost? Rationales for mandates have been: to eliminate adverse selection of certain services by having them elected by only those who need them; to correct for the undervaluing of certain services by employers (such as mental health services); and to provide a service at a lower cost by mandating a less-expensive provider, such as a psychologist instead of a psychiatrist. Arguments against are that mandates increase total plan costs and interfere in the negotiation of contracts between labor and management. One trend in certain larger companies (based on the premise that they do increase costs) has been to ignore mandates, an option open to a company that is self-insured. Increasingly, many larger companies are self-insured, while most individuals from smaller firms are enrolled in plans that are subject to state regulation.

Most studies do agree that mandates raise the cost of health insurance. Estimates are that mandated services account for between 18% and 21% of claim costs in Massachusetts and Maryland, while a different analytic technique estimated that mandates for chemical dependency treatment raise premiums for family coverage by 8.8%, psychologist visits by 11.8%, and coverage for psychiatric visits by 12.8% (Gabel & Jensen, 1989). Switching to self-insurance also raises premiums by 12.3%, although not adding certain mandated services may make this a fiscally sound approach for corporations in some states.

Most critical to a determination of how mandates affect access is whether such mandates discourage small employers from offering health insurance. A survey of small businesses that are part of the National Federation of Independent Businesses indicated that both mandates and state premium taxes on health insurance premiums reduced the likelihood that a firm would offer health insurance. Being in a state with taxes required to subsidize a risk pool reduced the likelihood of a small business offering health coverage by 10%; and, on average, new mandates decreased the likelihood of coverage from a small firm by 1.5% (Gabel & Jensen, 1989). Firms with more than 10 workers were more likely to continue coverage, despite mandates, than firms with fewer than 10 employees.

A more recent trend has been for states to expand health insurance coverage to all citizens. Several states have proposed comprehensive reforms, but many of these have not yet been implemented. More comprehensive proposals in Oregon and Minnesota will be discussed after reviewing state efforts at more modest coverage expansion. Hospitals have been major supporters of legislation designed to cover uncompensated care for hospitals. Two states that enacted such laws in the late 1980s were Massachusetts and Washington. The Washington plan was established in 1989 and funded through a state appropriation of $34 million to administer the plan, with no employer contribution required. Coverage was provided for people under 65 who earned less than twice the federal poverty level ($24,200 for a family of 4). The state expected to receive $8 million in premiums, with costs averaging $7.50 a month for an individual, and $36 to $45, depending upon location, for a family of four with an average income of $11,000, much less than comparable private insurance. It is estimated that more than 400,000 residents will qualify (Kenkel, 1989). Initial estimates are that the plan is having some success.

In 1986 Massachusetts implemented a more modest plan of an uncompensated care pool for paying hospitals. In addition, a more comprehensive plan was initially to be implemented in 1992. This has been delayed and will probably not be implemented. The uncompensated care pool has used a statewide hospital rate-setting commission. One study has examined the effectiveness of this reform for 1987, the year following its implementation, for one condition, acute myocardial infarction (heart attack) and whether the separate payment approach led to inequities in care actually received. While patients are receiving some care with the new state program, the pool patients are least likely to receive cardiac procedures and had substantially higher risks of death, as compared with fee-for-service and HMO patients (Young & Cohen, 1991).

A number of states are trying small-level reforms aimed at the insurance system. Vermont and Maine have enacted reforms to require the use of community rating (that is, to not price the insurance for certain small groups relative to characteristics such as age, sex, occupation, or health status, but use community-wide averages). The Vermont law applies to groups of 49 or fewer employees, and self-employed individuals, and prohibits rates based on health status. A gradual approach was adopted in Maine. Insurers must accept any group of fewer than 25 at a community rate, as of July 1993. Initially, up to 50% variation is allowed, based on age, sex, occupation, or geographic area, but this decreases to 0% over 5 years (Freudenheim, 1992). Oregon and Minnesota have also passed such laws as part of more comprehensive reforms.

Minnesota has forbidden basing rates on sex and limiting geographical variation in costs of insurance. In addition, the state is providing state-subsidized insurance for some uninsured middle-class Minnesotans. Basically, the Minnesota plan makes state-subsidized insurance available to all uninsured residents who are not eligible for Medicaid and whose incomes are less than 275% of the federal poverty level, currently $38,300 for a family of four. Those enrolled must have been without health insurance for more than 4 months and will pay premiums ranging from 1.5% to 10% of their income, depending upon current income. The program will be financed by increased cigarette taxes, a tax on the gross revenues of health care providers, and a tax on HMOs and Blue Cross-Blue Shield (BC-BS) in the state ("Minnesota approves," 1992). Given these taxes on health care, there was great opposition to the program from portions of the health care industry in the state.

Oregon has planned several major reforms. Because they are more comprehensive and include Medicaid, they require federal approval, unlike the Minnesota proposal that is to be implemented in 1993. The main thrust in Oregon is a health care rationing program. The initial draft passed in 1989 as Senate Bill 27, or the Oregon Basic Health Services Act, and would expand Medicaid eligibility to all persons below 100% of the federal poverty level. All such persons would receive the same benefits package, using a Health Services Commission to set priorities for Medicaid spending by ranking medical services (Grannemann, 1991). In addition, the act would require employers to cover workers and their dependents and would reform the small insurance market. Oregon has required that any group of 3 to 25 must be provided insurance at rates not more than 33% higher or lower than a midpoint.

In August 1991 the Oregon Department of Health Services submitted its proposal to the federal government (Eddy, 1991). The proposed plan ranked 709 services in order of priority for funding. This ranking was not arrived at lightly or in private. There were 11 public hearings held across the state; a survey of 1,000 Oregonians, in which they were asked to rank the importance of various procedures; and also a professional opinion arrived at by a special commission (Fox & Leichter, 1991). Care was divided into 366 essential services, 275 very important ones, and 68 valuable to certain individuals. The proposed plan would cover almost all basic essential services, such as treatment for acute conditions that can be fatal, maternity care, preventive care for children and adults, and comfort care for the terminally ill. Only eight essential services, such as liver transplantation for alcoholic cirrhosis of the liver, are excluded. Of the essential services, 19% are not covered, including several related to back and disc disorders, breast reconstruction, and surgery to correct congenital anomalies of the female genital organs. Only 5 of the third group of services are covered (Steinbrook & Lo, 1992).

What has been the response to this list in the health services community? Responses have ranged widely. Some groups are repulsed because explicit rationing of certain services is included. Others have criticized the list because the burden of some of the uncovered services may fall more heavily on certain groups, who already have broader coverage under the current Medicaid plan (children and women with young children). Some physicians have criticized the plan for not covering enough of the essential services (Steinbrook & Lo, 1992). Others have been critical of the degree of regulatory intrusion into clinical practice required to implement the priority list (Fischer, Welch, & Wennberg, 1992). An attempt by two social scientists to evaluate the proposal objectively mentioned their being impressed by the boldness of the proposal and the efforts to generate public discussion of the process (Fox & Leichter, 1991). Whether Oregon's plan will be approved by the federal government is still not clear, and one critic argues that it has too explicit a focus on rationing (E. B. Brown, 1991).

Lessons From Medicare

In 1988 and 1989 the U.S. Congress first passed and then repealed the Medicare Catastrophic Act of 1988, which provided an expansion of Medicare to provide catastrophic coverage for physician, hospital, and drug care. While the elderly were initially supportive of the proposal, the Congress (given concerns about the budget and trying to hold down the costs of the program) paid for most of the expansion of the program through higher Medicare Part B fees, which most elderly have deducted from their monthly Social Security checks, and through a surcharge on the income tax of those elderly wealthy enough to pay taxes each year. The elderly, especially middle- and high-income elderly whose taxes would have increased substantially and who would, in many cases, have had the highest effective tax rates in the country, reconsidered the attractiveness of this legislation and began to write their to legislators, suggesting repeal. After considerable debate, the House and Senate voted to repeal the extension.

What is the message of this for the health policy analyst? In public opinion polls of the elderly about health care, conducted over the past decade, most elderly are enthusiastic about expanding health care benefits but less certain about how to pay for them (Gabel, Cohen, & Fink, 1989). In a recent comment on health care cost burdens on the elderly, Rice (1989) demonstrated that Part B premiums, Medigap policies, and unassigned claims all led to an average cost per person of $915 in 1988 for the elderly. If the catastrophic extension had gone through as originally enacted, the typical elderly person in 1993 would have paid 20% of his or her income toward medical expenses. These figures indicate that the uproar over the program was not all unrealistic, although Americans have long had a tendency to be in favor of new programs as long as they do not cost them any money (Gabel et al., 1989). One message is that the elderly (and perhaps we can assume other age groups respond similarly on these issues) do not want to either see the increased cost of health care applied specifically to their own health care, or be easily singled out, as through a surcharge. Perhaps the most acceptable way to pay for expanded health care access is through general (and thus less visible) taxes and through taxes on employers, which are very hidden by the time they reach the consumer level. Another message may be that it is important for the U.S. health care system to consider both efficiency of care and providing the most care for our dollars, even if this requires changes in some aspects of health care delivery.

International Comparisons

Some international comparisons have already been discussed in other chapters. Among the important points are that most other countries spend a lower proportion of their GNP on health care and yet have as good or better health indicators. In addition, the role of administrative costs and the higher proportion of that component in the United States, as compared to a system such as the Canadian one, have also been discussed. One important factor in international comparisons is the willingness to accept constrained access or rationing. Depending on values around this issue, different analysts may arrive at different conclusions.

In the current debates, the countries whose systems are most often held to be potential models are such European countries as Great Britain, Germany, the Netherlands, and Sweden, along with our neighbor to the north, Canada. Overall political orientation and the values placed on preserving a role for private groups versus having a government-dominated system are important in determining the emphasis placed on a British model of government control versus a German/Dutch model of preserving a role for private groups (Kirkman-Liff, 1991; Kleig, 1991). The British system is the classic model of a governmental-controlled system, in which hospitals are owned by the state, and doctors are essentially employees of the state, although general practitioners actually contract with the government to provide care for a defined group of patients. Sweden also has a model dominated by the role of the state and state ownership of facilities. While the British system delivers an overall high quality of care, there is explicit rationing of some services and long waiting lists for elective procedures, which is how the government has traditionally held down costs. Sweden also has rationing, but has generally had a greater availability of hospital and surgical care. Great Britain has the lowest per capita spending on health of all major industrialized countries (Starfield, 1991). The amount of rationing in the British model has generally been viewed as unacceptable in an American framework.

In contrast, in somewhat different ways, both the Netherlands and Germany rely on a complex system of health insurance plans and contracting with groups of physicians and hospitals to provide health care services to their population. While there is universal coverage, it is achieved through a variety of nonprofit and for-profit insurers, not a single government agency. Both these countries have lower costs per capita than the United States and spend a lower proportion of their gross domestic product on health care (Kirkman-Liff, 1991).

Two recent articles have compared health care across 7 to 10 European and North American countries (Hurst, 1991; Starfield, 1991). In general, except for the United States, these countries have insured virtually all of their citizens. Most countries allow patients to select their own individual physician within some boundaries, and constrain medical expenses in a way acceptable to the polity. The cost of care is socially shared, so that, in essence, the rich help support the poor, the healthy help subsidize the sick, and the working-age population subsidizes the old (Hurst, 1991). Starfield compared 10 Western industrialized nations on the basis of three characteristics: extent of primary health care services, levels of 12 health indicators (such as life expectancy, infant mortality, and age-adjusted death rates), and satisfaction of the population in relation to overall costs. Ratings for the United States were low on all three indicators, while Canada, Sweden, and the Netherlands had generally high ratings on all three measures.

Probably the most frequent comparison in the past 10 years is between the U.S. system and Canada's. In essence, Canada has a provincially based single payor system for the major components of health care. There is variability from province to province in coverage of such things as drugs, dental care, and eye care, but all provinces provide a similar package of hospital and physician services. The system has worked well overall in controlling health care costs through the use of a single payor model and has relatively low administrative costs. There has been a recent spate of articles critical of the system and arguing that the United States would not achieve the same savings as the Canadians, due to increased demand or because estimates of the administrative savings are too great (Danzon, 1992; Neuschler, 1991; Sheils, Young,

& Rubin, 1992). A recent discussion of the United States/Canadian comparisons by two well-known Canadian health services researchers have concluded that those who oppose fundamental health care reform are trying to discredit the Canadian system as a way to derail movements toward reform in the United States (Barer & Evans, 1992). One such example they point to is gross misrepresentation of Canadian data in President Bush's recent health strategy documents. One recent article reviews data, arguing that the perception of relative cost control success in Canada arises from an inappropriate base of comparison (use of percentage of GNP or gross domestic product rather than real costs per capita) (Barer, Welch, & Antioch, 1991; Neuschler, 1991). The authors conclude that the Canadian single payor system has contained cost more effectively than the U.S. multi-payor system (the focus of the debate), while achieving more comprehensive access to care and better health outcomes (facts not generally debated), although they do point out that the system does include constrained access (or rationing) for certain services.

Comprehensive Proposals to Reform the U.S. System

A number of proposals have either been introduced at the federal level in the past several years or discussed among policy experts. It is very difficult to summarize all of the proposals, and specifics tend to change rapidly. What is more useful than to summarize specific proposals is to discuss broad general approaches and partially link those with some specific proposals. Among the major approaches under discussion or consideration are various versions of mandated care, some that focus on mandating that employers provide health insurance, and others that try to remove insurance from its close connection with employment. Many of these models would include multiple payors for care and multiple providers of care and still retain a place for the private health insurance companies. This approach is sometimes known as a managed competition or marketplace model. At the other extreme would be a universal program approach, in which there would be one payor for care and the simplicity of one set of benefits, either nationally or possibly regionally. To some extent, Medicare might be thought of as operating similarly to one version of this approach, but with the addition of stronger budget caps to control total costs. A third approach, intermediate between

Table 9.1 Models of Health Insurance Reform

Managed Competition, Mandates, Incremental	Pay or Play	Universal Program
Republican/Bush Plan	Pepper Commission	Physicians for a National Health Program
Medicaid Reform (not comprehensive)		Health USA
Enthoven Plan		

these two but which some experts believe would quickly become a single risk pool/single payor program, is the current notion of a pay or play approach. This is also related to the mandated approach because it would require the purchase of care by employers.

These approaches differ in the extent to which the goal is universal access; the ways in which they affect the uninsured and currently insured; costs to employers and the maintenance of a linkage with the employment system; relative costs, particularly of those that represent an insurance option versus a direct service option; and maintenance of a role for private health insurance companies. Some plans are better developed than others, and some have also received more sophisticated examinations by economists and policy experts in terms of projecting costs and impact on access. Depending upon the available material, each will be reviewed to some extent.

Mandated Approaches and Managed Competition

The Enthoven consumer choice health plan is a revision of a plan first proposed in 1980, which emphasized HMO-type plans and lots of consumer choice. The new version is definitely a managed competition plan, which would continue to rely on a system of qualified managed health care plans with a role for Medicare and Medicaid. The ultimate goal would be to transform the health care financing and delivery system, through voluntary action, into an array of managed care plans. Employers would have to cover their full-time employees and make a defined contribution equal to 80% of the cost of an average plan meeting federal standards and would have to offer a choice of health plans. To make people more cost-conscious, the tax-free employer contribution would be limited to that 80%. Employers would have to pay an 8% payroll tax on the first $22,500 of the wages and salaries of part-time seasonal employees, unless they were provided with a health insurance plan meeting federal requirements. Families with incomes below the federal poverty level would have all costs paid by the government. People with incomes between 100% and 150% of the federal poverty level would share the premium contribution on a sliding-scale basis. Self-employed persons, early retirees, and anyone else not covered through employment would be required to contribute through the income tax system (Enthoven & Kronick, 1991).

The third approach in this category was initially proposed by the Heritage Foundation in 1991 and is quite similar to the proposal suggested by Bush and the Republicans in 1992 (Butler, 1991). Because the Heritage Foundation proposal is more detailed, this discussion will follow its outline more closely. The heart of this plan is a tax reform strategy. The plan would eliminate the current tax exclusion for employer-provided health insurance and would break the connection between employment and insurance. Individuals would purchase private coverage from competing health insurance companies. There would be a tax credit for the insurance purchased, up to $1,250 for individuals and $3,750 for families of three or more, under the Bush version. Low-income families would receive from the government the amount required to purchase insurance. The plan would rely heavily on the tax treatment of the benefits to discourage overinsuring and overuse of care. There would be a requirement that plans offered would have to include a basic set of services to help people make appropriate choices about health insurance. A criticism of both this and the Enthoven plan is that they do not include strong cost-control features.

Pay or Play

The idea of pay or play has received a great deal of discussion nationally, and was partially the basis for reform proposed by Massachusetts in the late 1980s. Two different versions of this plan have received attention recently. One is a modification of the plan recommended by the Pepper Commission report (Rockefeller, 1991). The

Table 9.2 Health Care Reform Proposals

Author of Proposal	Coverage	Administration	Financing	Cost Containment/ Provider Reimbursement	Other Distinctive Features
Managed Competition, Mandates, Incremental					
Enthoven & Kronick	Universal	Private, Medicare, public sponsors	Employer/employee premium sharing; tax on employees & self-employed	Increased cost sharing, market forces, change tax deductibility of employer plans	Managed care system of delivery; no change in long-term care
Heritage Foundation/ Bush/Republican	Universal	Competing insurers; Medicare/Medicaid	Individual payment of all premiums or care; government pays for poor	Changes in tax treatment of health benefits to discourage overinsuring and overuse; reimbursement unchanged	Long-term care coverage at individual discretion
Pay or Play					
Rockefeller (Pepper)	Universal	Private: Insurers offer private plans. Government: replaces Medicaid with new program for poor nonworkers, and self-employed, with buy-in option for employed	Employer/employee premium sharing; existing government sources plus new taxes	Encourages use of managed care; cost sharing; improves consumers' knowledge; malpractice reform; public program pays Medicare rates; private insurance unchanged	Insurance reform; universal coverage of long-term care

continued

153

Table 9.2 Continued

Author of Proposal	Coverage	Administration	Financing	Cost Containment/ Provider Reimbursement	Other Distinctive Features
Universal					
Physicians for a National Health Program	Universal	Public administrator replaces Medicare, Medicaid, and private insurance	Payroll tax; existing government revenue sources; new taxes	Annual hospital budget negotiated based on past performance	Each state decides who runs plan; no copayments or deductibles; long-term care fully covered
Health USA (R. Brown)	Universal	Public administration by federal and state; use health plans	Federal and state health care funds; new payroll tax	MDs paid on negotiated fee schedule; negotiated state rates to hold down costs; hospitals on global budget	Separate health care from employment; use competing plans; retains private health insurer; long-term care coverage

SOURCE: Adapted from *JAMA*, May 15, 1991, vol. 265, pp. 2564-2565. © 1991, American Medical Association. Reprinted with permission.

other is a slight modification of the plan being proposed by the Senate Democratic leadership. The Pepper Commission plan would use a combination of incentives and requirements to guarantee that all workers and their nonworking dependents have insurance coverage through the job. There would be special tax credits and a 5-year subsidy to encourage small employers to provide health insurance. For those employers who could not afford even that, a new federal program, created to replace Medicaid, would cover all those not covered through the workplace, the poor, and the self-employed. Under the Senate Democratic version, employers who do not offer health insurance would pay about 7.5% of their payroll into a fund for the uninsured. A minimum benefit would be defined, and all employers would be required to offer it. There would be deductibles, with a total out-of-pocket limitation of no more than $3,000 in cost-sharing for any one family per year. Cost-sharing would be subsidized for low-income workers. Other features would be malpractice reform and coverage of long-term care.

Universal Payors

There are two different versions of universal plans that have received public discussion as well as written presentation in the literature. The most far-reaching plan was initially proposed by Physicians for a National Health Program (PNHP) and has been modified slightly in a 1991 version presented in the *Journal of the American Medical Association* (Grumbach, Bodenheimer, Himmelstein, & Woolhandler, 1991). The second plan was described by a health services researcher, Richard Brown, and was the basis of a Senate bill introduced by Senator Kerry of Nebraska (E. B. Brown, 1991).

The PNHP plan is modeled on the Canadian system. It would merge public and private health insurance programs into a single program. The government would control most aspects of health care, with hospitals paid on a negotiated schedule, and doctors according to a binding fee schedule. Money now spent for Medicare, Medicaid, and state and local care would finance the plan. In addition, there would be specific taxes on employees and employers. Patients could select their own doctors and hospitals, and all doctors would be members of the plan, though fees would vary some by geographic location. In one version, spending on health care would be limited to the same percentage of the GNP as in the year before the plan was adopted, as a way to restrain costs (Kenkel, 1989; Tolchin, 1989). The initial version of this plan was described in an article in the *Journal of the American Medical Association* (Woolhandler & Himmelstein, 1989). In a commentary in the October 1989 issue of the *Journal of the American Medical Association*, this plan was described as the northern light at the end of the tunnel (Woolhandler & Himmelstein, 1989). The plan was modified slightly in 1991 (Grumbach et al., 1991). It would include coverage for a full range of services, including long-term care services. While there is no question that the initial costs of this plan would be substantial, there is debate as to how much of the increased initial costs would not be a true cost, due to administrative savings and simplification of the system. More of the costs of health care under this proposal would be borne by taxation and less by out-of-pocket and individual premiums.

A second universal coverage plan has been introduced into Congress by Senator Bob Kerry of Nebraska. In contrast to the PNHP plan, this plan retains a role for various different delivery options and emphasizes the availability of different health care plans as providers, as opposed to a centrally run plan in the PNHP proposal (E. B. Brown, 1991). This plan would provide coverage to the entire resident population for comprehensive medical and preventive care and long-term care services. The federal government would contribute 87% of the program costs to each state, and states would set up a state health plan. Each individual in the state could enroll in the state plan or private plans. Approved plans would be paid a fee for each person in the state to whom they agree to provide care in that year. Hospitals would be financed through global budgets negotiated at the state level. Coverage would be separated from employment. Medicare and Medicaid would be folded into the overall plan, as would care to federal employees and veterans. The originators of the plan argue that, although the plan would cost $479 billion in its first year, the administrative savings and reductions in health costs would actually provide savings over 5 years. Thus, there would be funds to extend coverage to include long-term care benefits. A number of taxes would be increased, however, including the top rate of personal income taxes, the corporate rate, and some payroll taxes. Critics argue that the cost savings from administration are overestimated.

Will the United States Ever Enact
Fundamental Health Care System Reform?

Incremental Change Versus Fundamental Reform

What are viable strategies for dealing with access and uncompensated care problems in the future? Where is the United States heading by the year 2000? Will any of these plans be enacted, or will the United States continue to muddle through with its current health care system and small changes? The clamor for change appears to be growing, but all the proposed changes have different strengths and weaknesses. There appear to be two basic strategies that can be followed: completely restructuring the system, or incremental gap filling (Reinhardt, 1987; Tresnowski, 1992; Wilensky, 1987; Wilensky & Ladenheim, 1987). Based on past U.S. history of reforms in many areas, including health care, incremental gap filling is probably the most likely, although perhaps the least effective. The previous section has reviewed some of the major current national proposals, each of which purports to be a major solution. It is also very important to consider the controversy over the appropriateness of some rationing (often of more technological services) in a system versus limited access of some groups to basic care. None of the current plans explicitly discuss rationing, although global budgeting and use of tax funds generally lead to questions about total expenditures and how to allocate resources more quickly than other approaches might.

If incremental strategies are used, rather than any comprehensive reform approach, the strategies will need to address three different groups: the nonworking uninsured, the medically uninsurable, and the employed insured. Although not the majority of the uninsured, the nonworking uninsured include those people not eligible for Medicaid due to state limitations on income and categories of coverage, the homeless, and the deinstitutionalized mentally retarded. Minimum federal standards for Medicaid income eligibility, and the elimination of the link between categorical eligibility and the receipt of cash assistance, would be major improvements for those ineligible for Medicaid. A useful addition would be a transition program allowing some buy-in program for Medicaid for those above minimum levels, so that there is a continuum from extensive Medicaid coverage to completely unsubsidized coverage. This expansion could be an insurance-based mechanism, not direct payment to providers (Wilensky, 1987; Wilensky &

Ladenheim, 1987). Specially targeted programs that include direct payment to providers would probably be necessary for certain groups, such as the homeless and the mentally retarded, as well as groups of special health outcome interest, such as the high-risk prenatal care population.

How would this expansion be funded? Options are limited. One option is general tax revenues; others more linked to health care are a tax on hospital excise revenues or a premium tax on health insurance. Mullan (1987) argues that a strategy built on expanding Medicaid would need to establish a single agency of state government to assume responsibility for health care services of all types.

A second important group are those who are medically uninsurable. While probably less than 1% of the population, this group is important in terms of the large amount of health care it consumes. Fifteen states have tried to deal with this group through an insurance pool, with varying success. Some state programs have left people with such high co-payments and deductibles that the program still results in uncompensated care for facilities. A more comprehensive approach is one that targets the spending of some percentage of one's income (rather than a dollar amount) on health care and bears more similarity to a catastrophic health care approach. This has received little recent attention.

A very large group whose needs for health care must be addressed is the employed uninsured. The most likely incremental strategy is mandating of health insurance by employers, but at a lower level of coverage than in the comprehensive proposals already discussed. Minimal coverage might include some hospital coverage, perhaps with limited physician coverage. The lower the level of coverage, the more access to care remains a problem, although uncompensated care at the hospital level may be addressed. The higher the level of coverage, the more this solution resembles the more comprehensive approach. One recent suggestion involves an employer mandate to extend private sector coverage to the employed uninsured, while a second is a Medicaid buy-in that would subsidize public sector health insurance for the near poor (Thorpe, Siegel, & Dailey, 1989). A mandate that all firms offer health insurance to full-time workers would add 24.6 million people to the insured lists. These costs would be financed by the private sector but would affect the public sector. Estimates are of a $33-billion increase in insurance premium payments, and possible loss due to increased labor costs of 60,000 to 100,000 jobs. About 12 million people would still be uncovered, especially part-time workers, the unemployed, and their dependents.

One fairly simple approach to resolving some aspects of the access problem is to expand Medicaid eligibility to cover all persons with incomes below the federal poverty level. This would solve problems of variability by state in the program and would cost approximately $9 billion to $14 billion, depending on certain assumptions and extensions (Thorpe et al., 1989). Enrollment would increase the most in the Southern states. Savings to local governments would be about $1.3 billion in tax support of public hospitals. Uninsured workers with incomes slightly above the cut-off would have an incentive to work fewer hours and lower their incomes enough to become eligible.

Views of the Public

One change in the past 10 years is that the attitude of the U.S. public toward its health care system has become less positive. In a recent Harris poll that compared 10 nations, the U.S. public was the least satisfied about its health care (Barer & Evans, 1992). Another analysis of health polling data concluded that the U.S. public has decided that fundamental change is needed in the health care system (Blendon & Edwards, 1991). A substantial majority of Americans have indicated in public opinion polls that they favor a national health insurance plan financed through taxation (Blendon & Donelan, 1991).

There are also other indicators of dissatisfaction. Harris Wofford's Senate victory in Pennsylvania in the fall of 1991 was viewed partially as a public mandate in that state for major health care system reform. Yet serious attempts to reform the system have always failed, and the level of public debate has often degenerated into controversy among special interest groups about how to preserve their own positions, with the health insurance industry, hospitals, and physicians each concerned about their own stake in the system. Moreover, there are deep and fundamental disagreements within the American public about how to reform the system, with each individual very involved in making sure that his or her own health care access and quality would not suffer. One important aspect of this debate has been the acceptability of rationing or limited access to certain (often more technologically based) services.

Fundamental Reform: When Might It Occur?

How likely to be enacted are any of the more comprehensive approaches that would require restructuring the system? How different are the proposals? We have reviewed many different versions of national health care reforms, but the two most discussed within the American context are a universal one-payor system, similar to the Canadian system of comprehensive coverage while maintaining fee-for-service physicians (and now identified as the PNHP Program), and a market-based reform approach, such as the health plan advocated for the past 10 years by Enthoven (1980) and rediscussed recently as a consumer choice health plan for the 1990s (Enthoven & Kronick, 1991).

Reinhardt (1991) argues that if the United States ever adopts a comprehensive national health insurance system, it will come at the behest of a coalition of health care providers and a broad group of middle-aged, semi-impoverished, and politically articulate baby boomers. Until recently, many have argued that this was completely out of the bounds of likelihood. The recent public opinion data, some election results, and the growing concern of the business community about the impact of health care costs on American international competitiveness have expanded the discussion of reform. By 1989-1990, the idea of an expanded federal role and fundamental reform was again interesting to business leaders. Iacocca of Chrysler suggested looking at the European and Japanese systems as models, while *Newsweek* and many other popular sources have suggested the Canadian model (Waldman, 1989). Some younger physicians have begun to support fundamental change, including the plan based on the Canadian model (Grumbach et al., 1991). More conventional medical groups have also supported fundamental reform in the past few years. Arnold Relman, the former editor of the *New England Journal of Medicine*, speculated that by the end of the century we may be ready for a Canadian-type system (Tolchin, 1989).

One major help in answering the question as to whether and when the United States will achieve fundamental reform may come from an older article discussing threats to equity of health care in Great Britain, Canada, and the United States in the past. In that article, Weller and Manga (1983) discuss the concept of reprivatization of care. Reprivatization, they argue, involves shifting financial responsibility away from government and back to individuals through private health insurance schemes. It often also includes a value based on fee-for-service and freedom of choice for patients, and an acceptance of dual- or multi-tiered systems of care. They point out that the countries with the more extensive public programs have better records in stability of health expenditures and in mortality and morbidity. This does occur with the limitation of some rationing of services. Defects in the private sector and in piecemeal reform were demonstrated in Canada and Great Britain in earlier periods, leading to comprehensive reforms. Many of the current problems in those countries relate to delegation of too much power to physicians. In the United States, we are in a period of declining power of physicians and increased acceptance of government regulation in hospitals, through the DRG system, despite the 1980s rhetoric of less governmental intervention. A major question may be whether the United States can continue to afford the inefficiencies of its current multiple approaches to the provision of care. The administrative costs of provision of health insurance and complicated government programs to provide care (Medicare and Medicaid) appear to exceed costs of administration in many more centrally organized systems. United States companies spend 12% of premiums for overhead expenses, versus 3% in the Canadian system. United States physicians spend 45% of gross income for professional expenses, much of which is for billing, versus only 36% in Canada (Woolhandler & Himmelstein, 1989).

As Rashi Fein (1980), a well-known health economist, pointed out in a lecture in Great Britain almost a decade ago, efficiencies in neither access nor costs are achieved in the case of a dual market in health care. In this period of expansion of international contacts and a global economy, U.S. business may be unable to remain competitive while burdened with large health care costs beyond those borne by industry in competing countries. Moreover, the tolerance of the public for the current system appears to be declining, and interest in reform increasing. The incremental proposals for improving access all complicate health care provision while attempting to remove some inequities. A more comprehensive approach might well be cheaper and more equitable; however, such an approach would probably decrease provider control, might decrease the role of private health insurance companies and Blue Cross-Blue Shield, and would eventually involve some rationing for certain services. The built-in institutional interests and values against rationing may be too powerful to be overcome, especially if America can continue to afford its inefficiencies in health care. On the other hand, business leaders and the medical profession could provide a powerful push to consider a more efficient yet equitable health care system, moved along by public concerns. Both the economy and political changes will probably jointly hold the key to fundamental health care reform in the United States in the future.

References

Aday, L., Anderson, R., & Fleming, G. (1980). *Health care in the U.S.: Equitable for whom?* London: Sage.

Agency for Health Care Policy and Research (AHCPR). (1991). *Report to Congress: Progress of research on outcomes of health care services and procedures.* Washington, DC: Department of Health and Human Services.

Alspach, J. G. (1989). Registered care technologists: A case of medical myopia. *Clinical Care Nurse, 9,* 2, 10.

AMA still pushing RCT plan. (1991, April). *American Journal of Nursing, 91,* 110.

Andersen, M. L. (1983). *Thinking about women: Sociological and feminist perspectives.* New York: Macmillan.

Andersen, R., & Mullner, R. (1990). Assessing the health objectives of the nation. *Health Affairs, 9,* 152-162.

Aries, N., & Kennedy, L. (1990). The health labor force: The effects of change. In P. Conrad & R. Kern (Eds.), *The sociology of health and illness: Critical perspectives* (pp. 195-206). New York: St. Martin's.

Ball, J. K., & Turner, B. J. (1991). *AIDS in U.S. hospitals, 1986-1987: A national perspective* (AHCPR Pub. No. 91-0015. Hospital Studies Research Note 15, Agency for Health Care Policy and Research). Rockville, MD: Public Health Service.

Banta, D., Behny, C., & Wilems, J. (1981). *Toward rational technology in medicine.* New York: Singer.

Baquet, C., & Ringen, K. (1987). Health policy: Gaps in access, delivery and utilization of Pap smears in the United States. *Milbank Memorial Fund Quarterly 65,* [Supp.], 322-347.

Barer, M. L., & Evans, R. G. (1992, Spring). Perspective: Interpreting Canada: Models, mind set, myths. *Health Affairs, 11,* 44-61.

Barer, M.L., Welch, W. P., & Antioch, L. (1991). Canadian/U.S. health care: Reflections on the HIAA's analysis. *Health Affairs, 10,* 229-236.

Barnett, P. G., & Midling, J. E. (1989). Public policy and the supply of primary care physicians. *Journal of the American Medical Association, 262,* 2864-2868.

Beauchamp, D. E. (1980). *Beyond alcoholism: Alcohol and public health policy.* Philadelphia: Temple University Press.

Beland, F. (1987). Living arrangements preferences among elderly people. *The Gerontologist, 27,* 797-803.

Bergner, M., & Rothman, M. L. (1987). Health status measures: An overview and guide for selection. *Annual Review of Public Health, 8,* 191-210.

Binstock, R. H. (1991). From the Great Society to the aging society: 25 years of the Older Americans Act. *Generations, 15,* 11-18.

Blendon, R. J. (1990). Satisfaction with health systems in ten nations. *Health Affairs, 9,* 185-192.

Blendon, R. J., & Donelan, K. (1991). The public and the future of U.S. health care system reform. In R. J. Blendon & J. N. Edwards (Eds.), *System in crisis: The case for health care reform* (pp. 173-194). New York: Faulkner and Gray.

Blendon, R. J., Donelan, K., & Knox, R. A. (1992). Public opinion and AIDS: Lessons for the second decade. *Journal of the American Medical Association, 267,* 981-986.

Blendon, R. J., & Edwards, J. N. (1991). Conclusion and forecast for the system. In R. J. Blendon & J. N. Edwards (Eds.), *System in crisis: The case for health care reform* (pp. 269-278). New York: Faulkner and Gray.

Botehlo, R. J. (1991). Overcoming the prejudice against establishing a national health care system. In *Caring for the uninsured and underinsured* (pp. 146-154). Chicago: American Medical Association.

Bowen, O. R., & Burke, T. R. (1988, September). New directions in effective quality of care: Patient outcome research. *Federation of American Health Systems Review,* pp. 50-53.

Brook, R. H., Williams, K. N., & Davis-Avery, A. (1976). Quality assurance today and tomorrow: Forecast for the future. *Annals of Internal Medicine, 85,* 809-817.

Brown, E. B. (1991). Health USA: A national health program for the United States. *Journal of the American Medical Association, 267,* 552-558.

Brown, P. (1985a). Introduction. In P. Brown (Ed.), *Mental health care and social policy* (pp. 1-7). Boston: Routledge & Kegan Paul.

Burke, M. (1992, April 20). Hawaii's health care plan stirs Capitol Hill debate over access. *Hospitals, 16*(8), 32-36.

Butler, A. M. (1991). A tax reform strategy to deal with the uninsured. *Journal of the American Medical Association, 265,* 2541-2544.

Cascardo, D. (1982). Factors affecting cost containment in an HMO: A review of the literature. *Journal of Ambulatory Care Management, 5,* 53-63.

Case, T. W. (1991, November). Dying made easy. *National Review,* pp. 25-26.

Christensen, S. (1991). Did 1980s legislation slow Medicare spending? *Health Affairs, 10,* 135-142.

Christianson, J. B., Wholey, D. R., & Sanchez, S. M. (1991). State responses to HMO failures. *Health Affairs, 10*, 78-92.

Claiming success: AMA members vote to abandon the RCT idea. (1990, August). *American Journal of Nursing, 90*, 76-78.

Cleary, P. D., Devanter, N. V., Rogers, T. F., Singer, E., Avorn, J., & Pindyck, J. (1991). Trends in sociodemographic and behavioral characteristics of HIV antibody positive blood donors. *AIDS Education and Prevention, 3*, 60-71.

Cohodes, D. R. (1986). The home of the free, the land of the uninsured. *Inquiry, 23*(3), 227-235.

Colwell, J. M. (1992). Where have all the primary care applicants gone? *New England Journal of Medicine, 326*, 387-408.

Coward, R. T., & Cutler, S. J. (1989). Informal and formal health care systems for the rural elderly. *Health Services Research, 23*, 785-806.

Danzon, P. (1992, Spring). Hidden overhead costs. *Health Affairs, 11*, 21-43.

Davis, K., Gold, M., & Maleac, D. (1981). Access to health care for the poor. *Annual Review of Public Health, 2*, 150-182.

DeGeyndt, W. (1970). Five approaches for assessing the quality of care. *Hospital Administration, 15*, 21-42.

Delevan, S. M., & Koff, S. Z. (1990). The nursing shortage and provider attitudes: A political perspective. *Journal of Public Health Policy*, 62-80.

DesHarnais, S., Kobrinski, E., & Chesney, J. (1987). The early effects of the PPS on inpatient utilization and the quality of care. *Inquiry, 24*, 7-16.

Dienes, C. T. (1962). *Law, politics and birth control.* Urbana: University of Illinois Press.

Donabedian, A. (1968). Promoting quality through evaluating the process of patient care. *Medical Care, 6*, 181-202.

Donabedian, A., Wheeler, J. R., & Wyszewianski, L. (1982). Quality, cost and health: An integrative model. *Medical Care, 20*, 975-992.

Donovan, P. (1986). New reproductive technologies: Some legal dilemmas. *Family Planning Perspectives, 18*, 57-61.

Eddy, D. M. (1991). Oregon's plan: Should it be approved? *Journal of the American Medical Association, 266*, 2439-2445.

Edwards, W. O., & Fisher, C. R. (1989). Medicare physician and hospital utilization and expenditure trends. *Health Care Financing Review, 11*, 111-116.

Enthoven, A. (1980). *Health plan: The only practical solution to the soaring costs of medical care.* Reading, MA: Addison-Wesley.

Enthoven, A., & Kronick, R. (1989). Consumer choice health plan for the 1990s. *New England Journal of Medicine, 320*, 29-37.

Enthoven, A., & Kronick, R. (1991). Universal health insurance through incentives reform. *Journal of the American Medical Association, 265*, 2532-2536.

Ermann, D. A. (1990). Rural health care: The future of the hospital. *Medical Care Review, 47*, 33-74.

Estes, C. L., & Lee, P. R. (1986). Health problems and policy issues of old age. In L. Aiken & D. Mechanic (Eds.), *Applications of social science to clinical medicine and health policy* (pp. 335-338). New Brunswick, NJ: Rutgers University Press.

Evashwick, C. J. (1988). The continuum of long-term care. In S. J. Williams & P. R. Torrens (Eds.), *Introduction to health services* (3rd ed., pp. 212-254). New York: John Wiley.

Falk, I. S. (1983). Some lessons from the fifty years since the CMCC final report, 1932. *Journal of Public Health Policy, 4*, 135-161.

Fein, R. (1980). Social and economic attitudes shaping American health policy. *Milbank Memorial Fund Quarterly, 56*, 349-385.

Feldman, S. E., & Roblin, D. W. (1992). Standards for peer evaluation: The hospital quality assurance committee. *American Journal of Public Health, 82*.

Feldstein, M. (1971). The rising price of physicians' services. *Review of Economics and Statistics, 52*, 121-133.

Field, M. A. (1988). *Surrogate motherhood: The legal and human issues*. Cambridge, MA: Harvard University Press.

Fingarette, H. (1988). *Heavy drinking: The myth of alcoholism as a disease*. Berkeley: University of California Press.

Fischer, W.S., Welch, H. G., & Wennberg, J. E. (1992). Prioritizing Oregon's hospital resources. *Journal of the American Medical Association, 267*, 1925-1931.

Forrest, J. D. (1986). The end of IUD marketing in the United States: What does it mean for American women. *Family Planning Perspectives, 18*, 52-55.

Fox, D. M., & Leichter, H. M. (1991, Summer). Rationing care in Oregon. *Health Affairs, 10*, 7-21.

Fraser, I., Narcross, J., & Kralovec, P. (1991). Medicaid shortfall and total unreimbursed hospital care for the poor, 1980-1989. *Inquiry, 28*, 385-392.

Freeman, H. E., Blendon, R. J., Aiken, L. H., Sudman, S., Mullinix, C. F., & Corey, C.R. (1987, Spring). Americans report on their access to health care. *Health Affairs, 6*, 11-27.

Freidson, E. (1970). *Profession of medicine: A study of the sociology of applied knowledge*. New York: Dodd, Mead.

Freidson, E. (1987). The medical profession in transition. In L. Aiken & D. Mechanic (Eds.), *Applications of social science to clinical medicine and health policy* (pp. 63-79). New Brunswick, NJ: Rutgers University Press.

Freudenheim, M. (1992, April 26). On health insurance. *The New York Times*, p. E5.

Fried, M. G. (1990). *From abortion to reproductive freedom: Transforming a movement*. Boston: South End Press.

Fries, J. L., Green, L. R., Levine, S. (1989). Health promotion and the compression of morbidity. *Lancet, 482*, 895.

Fuchs, V. (1974). *Who shall live? Health, economics and social choice*. New York: Basic Books.

Fuchs, V. (1978). The supply of surgeons and the demand for surgical operations. *Journal of Human Resources, 13*, 33-56.

Gabel, J., Cohen, H., & Fink, S. (1989, Spring). Americans' views on health care. *Health Affairs, 6*, 11-27.

Gabel, J., & Jensen, G. (1989). *The price of state mandated benefits*. Paper presented at Association for Health Services Research Meeting.

Gay, G., Kronenfeld, J. J., Baker, S., & Amidon, R. (1989). An appraisal of organizational response to fiscally constraining regulation. *Journal of Health and Social Behavior, 30*, 41-55.

Gerstman, B. B., Gross, T. P., Kennedy, D. L., Bennett, R.C.X., Tomita, D. K., & Stadel, B. V. (1991). Trends in the content and use of contraceptives in the United States, 1964-88. *American Journal of Public Health, 81*, 90-96.

Gibson, R. M., & Waldo, D. R. (1981). National health Expenditures, 1980. *Health Care Financing Review, 3*, 1-54.

Ginzberg, E. (1987). A hard look at cost containment. *New England Journal of Medicine, 316*, 1153-1154.

Glaser, W. A. (1986). *Financing decisions in European health insurance*. New York: New School for Social Research, Graduate School of Management and Urban Professions.

GMENAC. (1980). *Report of the graduate medical education advisory committee to the secretary* (DHHS Report No. HRA 81-653). Washington, DC: U.S. Department of Health and Human Services.

Gold, R. B., & Daley, D. (1991). Public funding of contraceptive, sterilization and abortion services, fiscal year 1990. *Family Planning Perspectives, 23*, 204-211.

Golden, W. E. (1990). Entering the quality assurance decade. *The American Journal of the Medical Sciences, 33*, 178-180.

Goldstein, L. (1979). *The constitutional rights of women*. New York: Longman.

Grannemann, T. W. (1991). Priority setting: A sensible approach to Medicaid policy. *Inquiry, 28*, 300-305.

Gray, B. (1986). *For-profit enterprise in health care*. Washington, DC: National Academy Press.

Grumbach, K., Bodenheimer, T., Himmelstein, D. U., & Woolhandler, S. (1991). Liberal benefits, conservative spending. *Journal of the American Medical Association, 265*, 2549-2555.

Guterman, S., & Dobson, A. (1986). Impact of the Medicare prospective payment system for hospitals. *Health Care Financing Review, 7*, 97-114.

Haber, L. D. (1966). The epidemiology of disability: II. The measurement of functional capacity limitations. In U.S. Department of Health, Education and Welfare, Social Security Administration, *Social Security survey of the disabled, 1966*. Washington, DC: Government Printing Office.

Hadley, J., Steinberg, E. P., & Feder, J. (1991). Comparison of uninsured and privately insured hospital patients. *Journal of the American Medical Association, 265*, 374-379.

Haglund, C., & Dowling, W. L.. (1988). The hospital. In S. Williams & P. R. Torrens (Eds.), *Introduction to health services* (pp. 160-211). New York: John Wiley.

Harvard Medical Practice Study. (1990). *Patients, doctors and lawyers: Medical injury, malpractice litigation, and patient compensation in New York*. Cambridge, MA: Harvard University Press.

Haug, M. (1976). The erosion of professional authority: A cross-cultural inquiry in the case of the physician. *Milbank Memorial Fund Quarterly, 54*, 83-106.

Health Insurance Association of America. (1990). *Source book of health insurance data, 1990*. Washington, DC: Author.

Health-PAC. (1970). *The American health empire: Power, profits and politics*. New York: Vintage.

Henshaw, S. K., & Van Vort, J. (1990). Abortion services in the United States: 1987 and 1988. *Family Planning Perspectives, 22*, 102-108.

Hilts, P. J. (1990, December). Birth control backlash. *The New York Times Magazine*, pp. 41, 55, 70-72.

Himmelstein, D., & Woolhandler, S. (1986). Cost without benefit: Administrative waste in U.S. health care. *New England Journal of Medicine, 314*, 441-445.

Hing, E. (1987). *Use of nursing homes by the elderly* (Report No. 135). Hyattesville, MD: Government Printing Office, National Center for Health Statistics.

Hing, E., Sekscenski, E., & Strahan, G. (1989). *The national nursing home survey: 1985 summary for the United States*. [Vital and Health Statistics, Data From the National Health Survey, Series 13, no. 97]. Hyattesville, MD: Government Printing Office, National Center for Health Statistics.

Holahan, J., Hadley, J., Scanlon, W., & Lee, R. (1978). *Physician pricing in California* (Report No. 998-10). Washington, DC: Urban Institute Working Paper.

House Committee on Governmental Operations, Subcommittee on Human Resources and Intergovernmental Relations Report. (1988). *From back wards to back streets: The failure of the federal government in providing services for the mentally ill* (Report 100-641). Washington, DC: Government Printing Office.

Howard, E. F. (1991). Long-term care: On the comeback trail. *Generations, 15,* 31-34.

Hoy, E. W., Curtis, R. E., & Rice, T. (1991). Change and growth in managed care. *Health Affairs, 10,* 18-36.

Hsiao, W. C., Yntema, D. B., Braun, P., & Becker, E. (1988). Resource based relative values: An overview. *Journal of the American Medical Association, 260,* 2347-2353.

Hsiao, W. C., Yntema, D. B., Braun, P., & Becker, E. (1990). Refinement and expansion of the Harvard RBRVS. *American Journal of Public Health, 80,* 799-803.

Hurst, J. W. (1991, Fall). Reforming health care in seven European nations. *Health Affairs, 10,* 7-21.

Ingram, W. (1992). Assisted suicide—A change of heart. *Aging Today, 13,* 3.

Institute of Medicine. (1988). *Homelessness, health, and human needs.* Washington, DC: National Academy Press.

Institute of Medicine. (1989). *Controlling costs and changing patient care: The role of utilization management.* Washington, DC: National Academy Press.

Institute of Medicine. (1990). *Clinical practice guidelines: Directions for a new program.* Washington, DC: National Academy Press.

Jellinek, E. M. (1946). Phases in the drinking history of alcoholics. *Quarterly Journal of Studies on Alcohol, 7,* 1-88.

Jellinek, E. M. (1952). The phases of alcohol addiction. *Quarterly Journal of Studies on Alcohol, 13,* 673-684.

Joffe, C. (1991). Physician provision of abortion before Roe v. Wade. *Research in the Sociology of Health Care, 9,* 21-32.

Jogerst, G. J., & Dippe, S. E. (1981). Antibiotic use among medical specialties in a community hospital. *Journal of the American Medical Association, 245,* 842-846.

Jonas, S. (1992). *An introduction to the U.S. health care system* (3rd ed.). New York: Springer.

Kasper, J. D. (1987). The importance of type of usual source of care for children's physician access and expenditure. *Medical Care, 25,* 386-398.

Kellie, S. E., & Kelly, J. T. (1991). Medicare peer review organization preprocedure review criteria: An analysis of criteria for three procedures. *Journal of the American Medical Association, 265,* 1265-1270.

Kemper, P., Spillman, B., & Murtaugh, C. (1991). A lifetime perspective on proposals for financing nursing home care. *Inquiry, 28,* 333-344.

Kenkel, P. J. (1989, July 28). States move toward mandatory healthcare coverage to ensure that working poor are insured. *Modern Healthcare,* 36-43.

Kenkel, P. J. (1988). Managed care growth continued in 1987 despite companies' poor operating results. *Modern Healthcare,* 75-90.

Kiesler, C. A. (1982a). Mental hospitals and alternative care: Noninstitutionalization as potential public policy for mental patients. *American Psychologist, 37,* 349-360.

Kiesler, C. A. (1982b). Public and professional myths about mental hospitalization: An empirical reassessment. *American Psychologist, 37,* 1323-1339.

Kirkman-Liff, B. (1991). Health insurance values and implementation in the Netherlands and the Federal Republic of Germany. *Journal of the American Medical Association, 265,* 2496-2503.

Kleig, R. (1991). Risks and benefits of comparative studies. *Milbank Memorial Fund Quarterly, 69,* 275-291.

Kleinman, J. D., Gold, M., & Makuc, D. (1981). Use of ambulatory medical care by the poor. *Medical Care, 19,* 1011-1022.

Knowles, J. H. (1977). The responsibility of the individual. *Daedalus, 106,* 76-86.

Koch, A. L. (1988). Financing health services. In J. Williams & P. R. Torrens (Eds.), *Introduction to health services* (pp. 335-370). New York: John Wiley.

Kravitz, R. L., Greenfield, Rogers, S. W., Manning, W., Zubkoff, M., Nelson, E., Tarlov, A., & Ware, J. E. (1992). Differences in the mix of patients among medical specialties and systems of care: Results from the medical outcomes study. *Journal of the American Medical Association, 267,* 1617-1623.

Kronenfeld, J. J. & Whicker, M. L. (1984). *U.S. national health policy: An analysis of the federal role.* New York: Praeger.

Kronenfeld, J. J., & Whicker, M. L. (1990). *Captive populations: Caring for the young, the sick, the imprisoned and the elderly.* New York: Praeger.

Kutner, N. G. (1982). Cost-benefit issues in U.S. national health legislation: The case of the end stage renal disease program. *Social Problems, 30,* 51-64.

Kutner, N. G. (1990). Issues in the application of high cost medical technology: The case of organ transplantation. In P. Conrad & R. Kern (Eds.), *The sociology of health and illness: Critical perspectives* (pp. 358-372). New York: St. Martin's Press.

LaLonde, M. (1975). *A new perspective on the health of Canadians.* Ottawa, Canada: Information Canada.

Lamanna, M. A. (1991). Who makes the abortion decision: Law, practice and the limits of the liberal solution. *Research in the Sociology of Health Care, 9,* 9-20.

Lazerby, H. C., & Letsch, S. W. (1990). National health expenditures, 1989. *Health Care Financing Review, 12,* 1-26.

Levine, I. S., & Rog, D. R. (1990). Mental health services for homeless mentally ill persons: Federal initiatives and current service trends. *American Psychologist, 45,* 963-968.

Levit, K. R., Lazerby, S. W., Cowan, C. A., & Letsch, S. W. (1991b). National health care expenditures, 1990. *Health Care Financing Review, 13,* 29-54.

Levit, K. R., Lazerby, S. W., Letsch, S. W., & Cowan, C. A. (1991a). National health care spending, 1989. *Health Affairs, 10,* 117-139.

Lewin, T. (1992, March 15). Hurdles increase for many women seeking abortions. *The New York Times,* pp. 1, 11.

Linton, P. B. (1990). *Roe v. Wade* and the history of abortion regulation. *American Journal of Law and Medicine, 15,* 227-243.

Logerfo, J. P., & Brook, R. H. (1988). The quality of health care. In S. J. Williams & P. R. Torrens (Eds.), *Introduction to health services* (pp. 407-437). New York: John Wiley.

Lohr, K., & Schroeder, S. A. (1990). A strategy for quality assurance in Medicare. *New England Journal of Medicine, 322,* 707-712.

Lubitz, J., & Prihoda, R. (1983). *Use and costs of Medicare in the last years of life in health: United States and prevention profile.* Hyattesville, MD: Government Printing Office, National Center for Health Statistics.

Lurie, M., Ward, N. B., Shapiro, M. F., & Brook, R. H. (1984). Termination from MediCal: Does it affect health? *New England Journal of Medicine, 311,* 480-484.

Manton, K. G. (1990). Population models of gender differences in mortality, morbidity, and disability risks. In M. G. Ory & H. R. Warners (Eds.), *Gender, health and longevity: Multidisciplinary perspectives.* New York: Springer.

Manton, K. G., & Soldo, B. (1985). Dynamics of health change in the oldest old: New perspectives and evidence. *Milbank Memorial Fund Quarterly, 63,* 206-285.

Mayer, D. (1991, October 21). Limited class size at nursing schools baffles hospitals. *Health Week,* pp. 1, 31.

McCall, N., Knickman, J., & Bauer, E. (1991). Public/private partnerships: A new approach to long-term care. *Health Affairs, 10,* 164-176.

McCall, N., Rice, T., Boismier, J., & West, R. (1991). Private health insurance and medical care utilization: Evidence from the Medicare population. *Inquiry, 28,* 276-287.

McConnell, S., & Beitler, D. (1991). The Older Americans Act after 25 years: An overview. *Generations, 15,* 5-10.

McDowell, I., & Newell, C. (1987). *Measuring health: A guide to rating scales and questionnaires.* New York: Oxford University Press.

McIlrath, S. (1991a, October). AMA rejects RBRVS compromise. *American Medical News,* pp. 1, 39.

McIlrath, S. (1991b, November). Final RBRVS rules nearly finished. *American Medical News,* pp. 1, 31.

McIlrath, S. (1991c, December). HCFA issues final RBRVS rules. *American Medical News,* pp. 1, 26-47.

McIlrath, S. (1991d, December). RBRVS launch could be difficult. *American Medical News,* pp. 1, 37.

McKeown, T. (1979). *The role of medicine: Dream, mirage, or nemesis.* Princeton, NJ: Princeton University Press.

McKeown, T., & Record, R. G. (1955). Medical evidence related to English population changes in the eighteenth century. *Population Studies, 9,* 119-141.

McKeown, T., & Record, R. G. (1962). Reasons for the decline in mortality in England and Wales during the nineteenth century. *Population Studies, 16,* 94-122.

McKeown, T., Record, R. G., & Turner, R. D. (1975). An interpretation of the decline of mortality in England and Wales during the twentieth century. *Population Studies, 29,* 391-422.

McKinlay, J., & Arches, J. (1985). Toward the proletarianization of physicians. *International Journal of Health Services, 15,* 161-195.

McKinlay, J. B., & McKinlay, S. J. (1977). The questionable contribution of medical measures to the decline of mortality in the United States in the twentieth century. *Milbank Memorial Fund Quarterly/Health and Society, 5,* 405-428.

McKinlay, J. B., & Stoeckle, J. (1990). Corporatization and the social transformation of doctoring. In P. Conrad & R. Kern (Eds.), *The sociology of health and illness: Critical perspectives.* New York: St. Martin's Press.

McKinlay, S. M., & McKinlay, J. B. (1977). The questionable contribution of medical measures to the decline of mortality in the U.S. in the twentieth century. *Milbank Memorial Fund Quarterly/Health and Society, 55,* 405-428.

Mechanic, D. (1987). Correcting misperceptions in mental health policy: Strategies for improved care of the seriously mentally ill. *Milbank Memorial Fund Quarterly, 65,* 203-230.

Mechanic, D., & Rochefort, D. (1990). Deinstitutionalization: An appraisal of reform. *Annual Review of Sociology, 16,* 301-327.

Menken, M. (1991). Caring for the underserved: Health insurance coverage is not enough. In *Caring for the uninsured and underinsured* (pp. 107-110). Chicago: American Medical Association.

Miller, C. A. (1992). Wanting children. *American Journal of Public Health, 82*, 341-343.

Mills, D. H. (Ed.). (1977). *Report on the medical insurance feasibility study.* San Francisco: Sutter.

Minnesota approves major overhaul of health care system. (1992, April 19). *The New York Times*, p. 13.

Moccia, P. (1990). Toward the future: How could 2 million registered nurses not be enough? *Nursing Clinics of North America, 25*, 605-613.

Morrissey, J. P., Goldman, H. H., & Klerman, L. V. (1985). Cycles of institutional reform. In P. Brown (Ed.), *Mental health care and social policy* (pp. 70-98). Boston: Routledge & Kegan Paul.

Moscovice, I. (1988). Health care professionals. In S. J. Williams & P. R. Torrens (Eds.), *Introduction to health services* (pp. 308-334). New York: John Wiley.

Mosher, W. D. (1981). *Contraceptive utilization in the United States, 1976* (No. 7). [Vital and Health Statistics Series 23. Data from the National Survey of Family Growth] Washington, DC: Government Printing Office.

Mosher, W. D., & Pratt, W. F. (1990a). Contraceptive use in the United States, 1973-88. [Advance Data From Vital and Health Statistics of the National Center For Health Statistics] Washington, DC: Government Printing Office.

Mosher, W. D., & Pratt, W. F. (1990b). Use of contraception and family planning services in the United States, 1988. *American Journal of Public Health, 80*, 1132-1133.

Mowll, C. A. (1989, August). The search for solutions to the indigent care crisis. *Health Care Financial Management*, 19-25.

Moyer, M. E. (1989, Summer). A revised look at the number of uninsured Americans. *Health Affairs, 8*, 102-110.

Mullan, F. (1987, Spring). Poor people, poor policy. *Health Affairs, 6*, 113-117.

Mydans, S. (1990, November 4). Science and the courts take a new look at motherhood. *The New York Times*, p. 6.

National Center for Health Statistics. (1980). *Health United States*. Washington, DC: Government Printing Office.

National Center for Health Statistics. (1992, January 7). Advance report of final mortality statistics, 1989. *Monthly Vital Statistics Report, 40*.

Neuschler, E. (1991, Fall). Debating the Canadian system. *Health Affairs, 10 , 237-239.*

Newschaffer, C. J., & Schoeman, J. A. (1990). Registered nurse shortages: The road to appropriate public policy. *Health Affairs, 9*, 98-106.

Noelker, L. S., & Bass, D. M. (1989). Home care for elderly persons: Linkages between formal and informal caregivers. *Journal of Gerontology: Social Sciences, 44*, 63-70.

Nursing school enrollments up. (1992, January 27). *American Medical News*, p. 8.

Office of National Cost Estimates. (1990). National health expenditures, 1988. *Health Care Financing Review, 11*, 1-54.

Ory, M. G., & Duncker, A. P. (1992). *In-home care for older people.* Newbury Park, CA: Sage.

Ory, M. G., & Warners, H. R. (1990). *Health and longevity: Multidisciplinary perspectives.* New York: Springer.

Patrick, D. L., Bush, J. W., & Chen, M. N. (1973). Toward an operational definition of health. *Journal of Health and Social Behavior, 14*, 6-23.

Pepper Commission. (1990). *A call for action: U.S. bipartisan commission on comprehensive health care, final report.* Washington, DC: Government Printing Office.

Perrine, M., Peck, R., & Fell, J. (1989). Epidemiologic perspectives on drunk driving. *Surgeon General's workshop on drunk driving: Background papers* (pp. 33-36). Washington, DC: U.S. Department of Health and Human Services.

Petersdorf, R. G. (1992). Primary care applicants—They get no respect. *New England Journal of Medicine, 326,* 408-409.

Pincus, H. A. (1984). AIDS, drug abuse, and mental health. *Public Health Reports, 99,* 106-108.

Plough, A. L. (1986). *Borrowed time: Artificial organs and the politics of extending lives.* Philadelphia: Temple University Press.

Pollack, R. F. (1988). Serving intergenerational needs, not intergenerational conflict. *Generations, 12,* 14-18.

President's Commission for the Study of Ethical Problems in Biomedical and Behavioral Research. (1983, March). *Report: The ethical implications of differences in the availability of health services.* Washington, DC. Government Printing Office.

President's Commission on the Health Needs of the Nation. (1953). *Building America's health: Vols. 1 & 2.* Washington, DC: Government Printing Office.

Probst, J. C., Kronenfeld, J. J., Amidon, R., & Hussey, J. (1992, November). *Hospital closure in small rural counties.* Paper presented at American Public Health Association annual meeting.

Provencher, H. (1989). Registered care technologist. *The Canadian Nurse,* 27-28.

Public Health Service. (1979). *Healthy people: The Surgeon General's report on health promotion and disease prevention* (DHEW Pub. No. PHS 79-55071). Washington, DC: Government Printing Office.

Public Health Service. (1990). *Healthy people 2000: National health promotion and disease prevention objectives* (DHHS Pub. No. PHS 91-50212). Washington, DC: Government Printing Office.

Public Health Service. Department of Health and Human Services. (1990). *Healthy people 2000: National health promotion and disease prevention objectives* (DHHS Pub. No. PHS 91-50212). Washington, DC: Government Printing Office.

Regier, D. A., Boyd, J. H., Burke, J. D., Rae, D. S., Myers, J. K., Kramer, M., Robbins, L. N., George, L. K., Karno, M., & Locke, B. Z. (1988). One month prevalence of mental disorders in the U.S.: Based on five epidemiologic catchment area sites. *Archives of General Psychiatry, 45,* 977-986.

Reinhardt, U. E. (1991). Breaking American health policy gridlock. *Health Affairs, 10,* 96-103.

Renne, K. S. (1974). Measurement of social health in a general population. *Social Science Research, 3,* 25-44.

Reverby, S. (1990). A caring dilemma: Womanhood and nursing in historical perspective. In P. Conrad & R. Kern (Eds.), *The sociology of health and illness: Critical perspectives* (pp. 184-194). New York: St. Martin's Press.

Reynolds, W. J., Rushing, W. A., & Miles, D. L. (1974). The validation of a function status index. *Journal of Health and Social Behavior, 15,* 271-288.

Rice, T. (1989, Summer). Trading off access to enhance welfare. *Health Affairs, 8,* 96-101.

Rice, T. (1992). Containing health care costs in the United States. *Medical Care Review, 49,* 19-65.

Richardson, M. (1988). Mental health services: Growth and development of a system. In S. J. Williams & P. Torrens (Eds.), *Introduction to health services* (3rd ed., pp. 255-278). New York: John Wiley.

Rivas, E. E., & Torres-Gil, F. M. (1991). Politics, diversity, and minority aging. *Generations, 15*, 47-51.

Robert Wood Johnson Foundation. (1978). *Special report* (No. 1). [A new survey on access to medical care] Princeton, NJ: Author.

Robert Wood Johnson Foundation. (1983). *Special report* (No. 1). [Updated report on access to health care for the American people] Princeton, NJ: Author.

Robert Wood Johnson Foundation. (1987). *Special report* (No. 2). [Access to health care in the United States: Results of a 1986 survey] Princeton, NJ: Author.

Robinson, J. C. (1991). HMO market penetration and hospital cost inflation in California. *Journal of the American Medical Association, 20*, 2719-2723.

Rockefeller, J. D. (1991). A call for action: The Pepper Commission's blueprint for health care reform. *Journal of the American Medical Association, 265*, 2507-2511.

Rodman, H., Sarvis, B., & Bonar, J. W. (1987). *The abortion question.* New York: Columbia University Press.

Rosenbaum, R. (1991, May). Angel of death: The trial of the suicide doctor. *Vanity Fair, 54*, pp. 146-151, 203-211.

Rosenberg, C. E. (1987). *The care of strangers: The rise of the American hospital system.* New York: Basic Books.

Rosenblatt, R. (1992, January 19). How to end the abortion war. *The New York Times Magazine*, pp. 26, 41-42, 50, 56.

Rosenblatt, R., & Moscovice, I. (1982). *Rural health care.* New York: John Wiley.

Rosenblatt, R. A. (1992). Specialists or generalists: On whom should we base the American health care system? *Journal of the American Medical Association, 267*, 1665-1666.

Ross, J. W. (1990, September/October). Considering the other edge of life. *Hastings Center Report*, pp. 46-48.

Rossi, P., Wright, J. D., Fischer, G. A., & Willis, G. (1987). The urban homeless: Estimating composition and size. *Science, 235*, 1336-1341.

Roth, D., Bean, G. L., & Hyde, P. S. (1986). Homelessness and mental health policy: Developing an appropriate role for the 1980s. *Community Mental Health Journal, 22*, 203-214.

Roth, J. A. (1991). A sour note on Roe v. Wade. *Research in the Sociology of Health Care, 9*, 3-8.

Rothman, B. K. (1989). *Recreating motherhood: Ideology and technology in patriarchal society.* New York: Norton.

Rothman, D. (1971). *The discovery of the asylum.* Boston: Little, Brown.

Russell, L. B. (1986). *Is prevention better than cure?* Washington, DC: Brookings Institution.

Ryder, N. B., & Westoff, C. F. (1971). *Production in the U.S., 1965.* Princeton, NJ: Princeton University Press.

Salive, M. E., Mayfield, J. A., & Weissman, N. W. (1990). Patient outcomes research teams and the Agency for Health Care Policy and Research. *Health Services Research, 25*, 697-707.

Schieber, G. J., & Poullier, J. P. (1991). International health spending: Issues and trends. *Health Affairs, 10*, 106-16.

Schlenger, W. E. (1976). A new framework for health. *Inquiry, 13*, 207-214.

Scull, A. T. (1985). Madness and segregative control: The rise of the insane asylum. In P. Brown (Ed.), *Mental health care and social policy* (pp. 17-40). Boston: Routledge & Kegan Paul.

Shadish, W. R., Lurigo, A. J., & Lewis, D. A. (1989). After deinstitutionalization: The present and future of mental health long term care policy. *Journal of Social Issues, 45*, 1-15.

Sheils, J. F., Young, G. J., & Rubin, R. J. (1992, Spring). O Canada: Do we expect too much from its health care system? *Health Affairs, 11,*7-20.

Sherlock, D. B. (1986) Indigent care in rational markets. *Inquiry, 23*, 261-267.

Siu, A., Sonnenberg, F. A., Manning, W. G. (1986). Inappropriate use of hospitals in a randomized trial of health insurance plans. *New England Journal of Medicine, 315*, 1259-1266.

Somerville, J. (1992, February 10). Fewer Americans covered by employer insurance. *American Medical News*, pp. 3, 27.

Sprague, J. (1991, August). *The reproductive debate.* Paper presented at the American Sociological Association meeting, Cincinnati, OH.

Starfield, B. (1991). Primary care and health. *Journal of the American Medical Association, 266*, 2268-2271.

Starr, P. (1982). *The social transformation of America medicine.* New York: Basic Books.

Steinbrook, R., & Lo, B. (1992). The Oregon Medicaid demonstration project. *New England Journal of Medicine, 326*, 340-344.

Stevens, R. (1989). *In sickness and in wealth: American hospitals in the twentieth century.* New York: Basic Books.

Stone, R. (1986, September 30). Aging in the eighties: Age 65 years and over, use of community services [Advance Data from Vital and Health Statistics Series, No 124]. Hyattesville, MD: Government Office, National Center for Health Statistics.

Stoto, M., & Durch, J. (1991). National health objectives for the year 2000: The demographic impact of health promotion and disease prevention. *American Journal of Public Health, 81*, 1456-1465.

Sulloway, A. W. (1959). *Birth control and Catholic doctrine.* Boston: Beacon.

Tell, E. J., Cohen, M., Larson, M. J., & Batten, H. (1987). Assessing the elderly's preferences for lifecare retirement options. *The Gerontologist, 27*, 503-509.

The second 100,000 cases of acquired immunodeficiency syndrome—United States. (1992). *Journal of the American Medical Association, 267*, 788.

The U.S. contraceptive gap. (1991). *Medicine and Health Perspectives* [Supp. to May 13, 1991], 1-4.

Thorpe, K. E., Siegel, J. E., & Dailey, T. (1989). Including the poor. *Journal of the American Medical Association, 261*, 1003-1007.

Todd, J. S., Seekins, S. B., Kirchbaum, J., & Harvey, L. (1990). Health access America—Strengthening the U.S. health care system. *Journal of the American Medical Association, 265*, 2503-2506.

Tolchin, M. (1989, September 24). Sudden support for national health care. *The New York Times*, p. E4.

Torrens, P. R. (1988). In S. J. Williams & P. R. Torrens (Eds.), *Introduction to health services* (3rd ed., pp. 3-32). New York: John Wiley.

Tresnowski, B. R. (1992). The '92 elections. *Inquiry, 29*, 5-6.

U.S. Bureau of the Census. (1986a). *Statistical abstract of the United States, 1987.* Washington, DC: Government Printing Office.

U.S. Bureau of the Census. (1986b). *Current population survey.* Washington, DC: Government Printing Office.

U.S. Congress, Senate Special Committee on Aging. (1988). *The rural health care challenge* (Report 100-145). Washington, DC: Government Printing Office.

U.S. Department of Health, Education and Welfare. (1980). *The national nursing home survey: 1977 summary for the United States* (DHEW Pub. No. PHS 79-1794). Washington, DC: Government Printing Office.

U.S. Senate Special Committee on Aging. (1988). *Aging America: Trends and projection.* Washington, DC: Government Printing Office.

Waldman, S. (1989, August 28). Biting the insurance bullet. *Newsweek,* p. 46.

Waldo, D. R., Levit, K. R., & Lazerby, H. (1986). National health expenditures, 1985. *Health Care Financing Review, 8,* 1-21.

Wann, M. (1990, July). Hospital reluctance to offer abortions hits rural areas hard. *Health Week News,* pp. 12.

Weiner, J. (1989). Forecasting physician supply: Recent developments. *Health Affairs, 8,* 173-179.

Weiss, J. A. (1990) Ideas and inducements in mental health policy. *Journal of Policy Analysis and Management, 9,* 178-200.

Weller, G. R., & Manga, P. (1983, Fall). The push for reprivatization of health care services in Canada, Great Britain, and the United States. *Journal of Health Politics, Policy and Law, 8,* 495-518.

Wells, K. B., Stewart, A., & Hays, R. D. The functioning and well-being of depressed patients: Results from the medical outcomes study. *Journal of the American Medical Association, 262,* 914-919.

Whicker, M. L., & Kronenfeld, J. J. (1986). *Sex role changes: Technology, politics, and policy.* New York: Praeger.

Wildavsky, A. (1977). Doing better and feeling worse: The political pathology of health policy. In J. H. Knowles (Ed.), *Doing better and feeling worse: Health in the U.S.* (pp. 105-123). New York: Norton.

Wilensky, G. R. (1987). Viable strategies for dealing with the uninsured. *Health Affairs, 6,* 33-40.

Wilensky, G. R., & Ladenheim, K. E. (1987, Winter). The uninsured. *Frontiers of Health Services Management, 4,* 3-31.

Williams, R.G.A., Johnston, M., Willis, L. A., & Bennett, A. E. (1976). Disability: A model and measurement technique. *Journal of Epidemiology and Community Health, 30,* 71-78.

Wilson, R. W., & White, E. L. (177). Changes in morbidity, disability, and utilization differences between the poor and the nonpoor. *Medical Care, 15,* 636-650.

Wolinsky, F. D., Aguirre, B. E., & Fans, L. J. (1989). Ethnic differences in demand for physician and hospital utilization among older adults in major American cities. *Milbank Memorial Fund Quarterly, 67,* 412-449.

Woolhandler, S., & Himmelstein, D. U. (1989). A national health program: Northern light at the end of the tunnel. *Journal of the American Medical Association, 262,* 2136-2137.

Woolhandler, S., & Himmelstein, D. U. (1991). The deteriorating administrative efficiency of the U.S. health care system. *New England Journal of Medicine, 324,* 1253-1258.

World Health Organization (WHO). (1958). *The first ten years of the World Health Organization.* Geneva: World Health Organization.

Wright, J. D. (1989). *Address unknown: The homeless in America. New York: Aldine.*
Young, G. J., & Cohen, B. B. (1991). Inequities in hospital care. The Massachusetts experience. *Inquiry, 28,* 255-262.
Zola, I. (1990). Medicine as an institution of social control. In P. Conrad & R. Kerns Eds.), *Sociology of health and illness: Critical perspectives* (pp. 398-408). New York: St. Martin's Press.

Author Index

Subject Index

182

About the Author

Jennie Jacobs Kronenfeld is a Professor in the School of Health Administration and Policy, Arizona State University. She holds a doctorate (1976) and a master's degree (1973) in sociology from Brown University, and a master's degree (1971) in sociology and history from the University of North Carolina. Prior to coming to Arizona, she held faculty positions at the University of Alabama in Birmingham and the University of South Carolina.

She has published more than 80 articles and book chapters on public health, medicine, health services research, and sociology. She has co-authored four books: on the social and economic impact of coronary artery bypass surgery (1981); on the federal role in health policy (1984); on the impact of technology on sex roles and social change (1986); and on public versus private models of service delivery in several different human services areas, including health (1990). Her current research interests include health policy issues, especially access to health care and reform of the health care system, and research on preventive aspects of health care such as perceptions of risk, childhood injury, and the relationship between social roles and wellness.